THE *Sunset*
APPETIZER BOOK

**By the editors
of Sunset Books
and Sunset Magazine**

LANE BOOKS · MENLO PARK, CALIFORNIA

ABOUT APPETIZERS

It may be a cocktail party, a reception, an informal get-together of a few friends, a holiday open house. No matter what the occasion for the party, however, some appetizing morsels of food are always in order. How many they will be and in what variety depends upon the type of party.

If dinner is to follow shortly, one or two really tempting appetizers, offered in small quantity, will suffice; in fact, no more *should* be served if your guests are to appreciate your culinary efforts. The dinner party, incidentally, presents a wonderful opportunity to serve an elegant first-course appetizer—the impressive dishes that in Europe go by such names as *hors d'oeuvre, antipasto,* or *zakuski.*

If, on the other hand, your party is an open-end affair that is likely to last for several hours, your guests will be craving more substantial fare: chafing dish specialties; skewered appetizers broiled over a *hibachi* or an outdoor barbecue; spicy meat balls simmering in a casserole over a candle warmer.

In the pages that follow are all kinds of appetizers—hot ones, cold ones, canapés, first courses, dips and spreads, sea food cocktails and fruit cocktails. We've even included a few choice appetizer beverages and some very special party punches and coolers. All have been tested in the Sunset kitchens, given high ratings by cautious taste panels, and published in Sunset Magazine. Select those that please you. Present them in your most attractive and unusual serving dishes. Add a friendly combination of people, your own warm welcome, a festive setting—and you have the ingredients for a party that should be a smashing success.

First Printing September 1965

CONTENTS

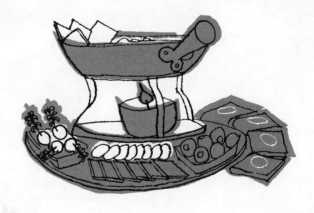

You'll get compliments when you serve spicy Korean Style Beef Cubes (page 18).
If you live near an Oriental market, get black sesame seed for unique flavor; other-
wise, use regular sesame seed, toasted.

HOT APPETIZERS
Irresistible treats hot from the oven

Water Chestnut Appetizers

This combination of crisp bacon, salty soy sauce, and crunchy water chestnuts makes an ideal hors d'oeuvre.

1 can (5 oz.) water chestnuts, drained
¼ cup soy sauce
¼ cup sugar
4 slices bacon, each cut in half crosswise and lengthwise

Marinate water chestnuts in soy for 30 minutes. Roll each chestnut in sugar, then wrap with a strip of bacon and secure with a cocktail pick. Arrange on a cake rack in a shallow pan or on broiler. Bake in a hot oven (400°) for 20 minutes. Drain on paper toweling.

Before serving, return to a moderate oven (350°) for about 5 minutes to reheat and crisp the chestnuts. These are best when made in the morning and reheated. Makes about 16 appetizers.

Glazed Ham Cubes

This appetizer takes only minutes to prepare; it is best if served hot from the broiler.

1 large sliced cooked ham, ½ inch thick
⅓ cup chunk-style peanut butter

Spread ham with peanut butter. Put under the broiler for 2 to 3 minutes or until the peanut butter forms a brown crust. Place the ham slice on a cutting board and cut it in 1-inch squares. Serve on toothpicks. Makes about 50 appetizers.

French-fried Mushrooms

This hot appetizer is cooked and served on long bamboo skewers. To save yourself last minute work, prepare French-fried mushrooms ahead of time and cook them quickly before serving.

3 dozen fresh mushrooms, each about 1 inch in diameter
2 eggs
1 teaspoon salt
Few grindings of pepper
Flour
Fine cracker crumbs
Salad oil or shortening for deep frying

Sauce:
½ cup sour cream
½ cup mayonnaise
1 tablespoon minced dill pickles
1 tablespoon chopped capers
1 minced fillet of anchovy

Remove mushroom stems (save them for soup or sauces). Impale each cap on a long bamboo stick, inserting the point from edge to edge. Beat eggs together with salt and pepper. Holding onto the ends of bamboo sticks, swish caps through flour, then through seasoned beaten egg, then through fine cracker crumbs. Let dry while you heat deep fat to 360°. Fry mushrooms for 4 minutes, or until brown. You can use the bamboo sticks for turning and removing the caps.

Serve at once with sauce made by combining sour cream, mayonnaise, pickles, capers, and anchovy. Makes 36 appetizers.

Your guests won't be able to resist these attractive Barbecued Prawns—a good appetizer for a patio party.

Fried Ginger Pork

This wonderful pork appetizer is prepared in Oriental style. It lends itself especially well to a barbecue.

2 pounds boneless fresh pork shoulder, cut in 1-inch cubes
¼ cup oil (sesame, peanut, or other bland oil)
1 cup finely minced onion
1 large clove garlic, crushed
½ cup soy sauce
1 tablespoon chopped fresh ginger mixed with 1 teaspoon sugar, or 1 tablespoon chopped preserved or crystallized ginger
2 tablespoons vinegar

Brown pork thoroughly on all sides in oil. Add onion and garlic. Cook until onion becomes soft, then add soy sauce, ginger, and vinegar. Cover pan and let simmer for about 10 minutes, or until the pork is done. Serve on toothpicks, right from the pan in which you've cooked it. Makes 3 to 4 dozen appetizers.

Barbecued Prawns

Prawns are always a favorite appetizer. Your only problem is to keep the tray replenished.

2 pounds medium-sized raw prawns, peeled and deveined
1 can tomato sauce
½ cup molasses
1 teaspoon dry mustard
Salt
Pepper
Liquid hot-pepper seasoning to taste
¼ cup oil
Pinch of thyme

Marinate prawns in a mixture of tomato sauce, molasses, dry mustard, salt, pepper, liquid hot-pepper seasoning, oil, and thyme. Ten minutes before serving, broil on both sides, basting often. Makes about 50 appetizers.

Cottage Cheese Rounds

These pale gold flaky rounds have a surprise ingredient—cottage cheese. You can make them ahead, and bake just before serving.

1 cup regular all-purpose flour
½ cup soft butter or margarine
1 cup small curd cottage cheese
1 teaspoon salt
1 egg yolk, beaten

Sift flour, measure, and combine in a bowl with butter, cottage cheese, and salt. Mix thoroughly with a spoon until well blended. Shape into a ball, place on a lightly floured board, and knead about 10 times. Roll ½-inch thick and cut in rounds 2 inches in diameter (or smaller, if you like). Brush tops with egg yolk. Place on a greased baking sheet and bake in a very hot oven (450°) for 12 to 15 minutes or until lightly browned. Serve hot. Makes about 18 appetizers.

Fondue Bourguignonne: tender morsels of beef, cooked in butter and oil, then dipped in sauce.

Fondue Bourguignonne

Guests cook their own skewered meat and dip each chunk into the sauce of their choice. The basic recipe calls for beef tenderloin, but you can also use liver, kidney, sweetbreads, chicken breast, lamb, large peeled and deveined shrimp, or fish cubes. Serve just one or several, but do not cook meat and fish in the same fat.

About 5 pounds beef tenderloin
Butter
Cooking oil
2 dozen French rolls, sliced

Cut meat into one-bite chunks and heap, uncooked, into serving bowls. Put 1½ inches melted butter and cooking oil in equal parts into electric saucepan, frying pan, or chafing dish with good heating element. Arrange with meat, skewers or fondue forks, a selection of sauces (recipes follow), and a platter of French roll slices. During party, keep fat hot (about 210°); meat will take only a couple of minutes to cook. Makes enough to serve 50 along with other food.

Mock Béarnaise Sauce: Soak 2 teaspoons dried tarragon in 2 tablespoons tarragon vinegar. Add 2 cups mayonnaise, ¼ teaspoon dry mustard, and 6 peeled shallots or green onions. Whirl in blender.

Anchovy Sauce: Add 2 tablespoons (or more, to taste) anchovy paste to 2 cups mayonnaise; mix well.

Garlic Sauce: Cream 1 pound soft butter with 2 puréed cloves garlic; add cayenne or Worcestershire to taste.

Sour Cream Sauce: Add 2 tablespoons paprika and ¼ cup very finely minced onion to 2 cups sour cream. Add salt to taste. Dill weed may be used instead of paprika.

Mustard Sauce: Combine 2 cups mayonnaise, 2 tablespoons tarragon vinegar, and 3 tablespoons dry mustard. Mix well and add salt to taste.

Curry Sauce: Combine 2 tablespoons curry powder, 1 puréed clove garlic, 1 tablespoon lemon juice, and 2 cans (10½ oz. each) beef gravy. Correct seasoning, adding salt if needed. Heat; serve over candle warmer.

Rosemary Walnuts

Rosemary is used to flavor these roasted walnut appetizers.

2 tablespoons melted butter
1½ teaspoons crumbled rosemary
1½ teaspoons salt
¼ to ½ teaspoon cayenne
2 cups walnut halves

Mix together butter, rosemary, salt, cayenne, and walnut halves. Pour into a shallow pan, spreading nuts in a single layer. Roast until richly browned in a moderate oven (350°) shaking occasionally; takes about 10 to 15 minutes. Serve hot (or reheat in oven) as an appetizer.

Sherried Shrimp with Tangy Sauce

Here you marinate shrimp in sherry, and then cook the shrimp and keep them warm while they are being served. Your guests dip them in a special sauce.

1½ pounds raw shrimp or prawns, peeled and deveined
¼ cup dry sherry
¼ cup (⅛ lb.) butter
½ teaspoon garlic salt
¼ cup grated Parmesan cheese

Place shrimp in a bowl and pour sherry over them. Let marinate for several hours. Melt butter in frying pan over low heat. Add shrimp and sherry. Sprinkle with garlic salt and simmer for 10 to 15 minutes. Just before serving, sprinkle cheese over shrimp, and place under broiler for 2 to 3 minutes until cheese is lightly browned. Serve hot with Tangy Sauce (recipe below). Makes appetizers for 6 to 8 people.

Tangy Sauce:
½ cup mayonnaise
2 teaspoons lemon juice
1 tablespoon catsup
2 teaspoons Worcestershire
2 teaspoons prepared mustard

Thoroughly mix together mayonnaise, lemon juice, catsup, Worcestershire, and prepared mustard. Refrigerate until ready to use. Makes about ½ cup sauce.

Tiny shrimp turnovers flavored with parsley butter— a tempting addition to an hors d'oeuvre assortment.

Shrimp in Pastry

Crescent-shaped pastry turnovers with a shrimp filling are surprise tidbits for a display of hors d'oeuvres. Bake just before serving so they will be piping hot.

15 medium-sized shrimp or prawns
Pastry that calls for 1½ cups flour, made from your favorite recipe

Parsley butter:
2 tablespoons butter
1 tablespoon minced parsley
½ teaspoon salt
½ teaspoon garlic salt

If using raw shrimp, cook, peel, and devein. Cut in half crosswise and set aside. Make pastry; before rolling out pastry, make up parsley butter by mixing butter, parsley, salt, and garlic salt. Cut out pastry rounds with a biscuit cutter. Place halved prawns on the pastry rounds. Brush them with parsley butter, fold over pastry, and seal well. Bake in a very hot oven (450°) for 8 to 10 minutes. Makes 30 appetizers.

Empanaditas

You will not need to worry about whether your guests care for tongue when you serve these empanadas. They won't suspect its presence in the unusual and well-flavored filling.

Pastry
1 medium-sized onion, chopped
3 tablespoons shortening or salad oil
1 cup finely chopped cooked tongue
½ cup raisins
1 cup chopped ripe olives
½ teaspoon salt
¼ cup sugar
¼ cup sweet wine or fruit juice

Prepare pastry, using your own recipe based on 2 cups flour or a pie crust mix for a double crust pie. Roll out ⅛ inch thick, and cut into 3-inch circles. Spoon filling on one side of circle. Dampen edges of dough, and fold over; press edges together securely with fork. Bake in moderately hot oven (375°) for 15 to 20 minutes, or until browned.

Filling: Sauté onion in shortening or oil. Add all the remaining ingredients and simmer until thickened (about the consistency of mincemeat). Cool before using. Makes about 36 appetizers.

Spicy Cocktail Wieners

This couldn't be easier!

1 jar (6 oz.) prepared mustard
1 jar (10 oz.) red current jelly
1 pound frankfurters, cut in bite-size pieces

Heat over hot water the prepared mustard mixed with red currant jelly. Add frankfurters and heat through. Serve hot from a chafing dish, electric frying pan, or shallow saucepan. Spear with toothpicks to eat. Makes 8 to 10 servings.

Cubes of garlic-flavored pork, baked until crisp and browned, reheated at serving time in a chafing dish.

Garlic Pork Nuggets

Serve these rich, crispy chunks of pork to eat plain or dipped in taco sauce (the bottled kind is very good). Pork shoulder is a good cut to use for this dish.

5 pounds lean pork
1 tablespoon salt
Freshly ground pepper
3 cloves garlic, puréed

Cut pork into 1-inch cubes; mix thoroughly with salt, pepper, garlic. Spread in layers in shallow baking pans, and bake in a moderate oven (350°) for 1 hour. Stir occasionally and drain off fat accumulations. When serving, reheat about a pound at a time in the oven (or in the chafing dish if it has a good heating element); serve in chafing dish. Makes enough for about 50 people.

Stuffed Broiled Mushrooms

Here's a canapé that's good for many occasions. The mushrooms are served on rounds of crisp toast so your guests won't get greasy fingered.

24 mushrooms with caps about 1 inch in diameter
¼ pound small mushrooms
1 or 2 green onions
1 piece of sharp Cheddar cheese, about the size of an egg
1 teaspoon Worcestershire
Dash of liquid hot-pepper seasoning
½ teaspoon salt
½ teaspoon pepper
¼ teaspoon garlic salt
Very small pinch of mixed Italian herbs
3 tablespoons dry bread or cracker crumbs
¼ cup (⅛ lb.) butter
Dash of liquid hot-pepper seasoning
½ teaspoon Worcestershire
Paprika

Clean and stem 1-inch mushrooms and set caps aside. Clean small mushrooms. Then chop very fine and mix together the large mushroom stems, the small mushrooms, the onions, and the cheese. Add the 1 teaspoon Worcestershire, a dash of liquid hot-pepper seasoning, salt, pepper, garlic salt, mixed Italian herbs, and bread or cracker crumbs.

Melt the butter and add the second dash of liquid hot-pepper seasoning and the ½ teaspoon Worcestershire. Put ½ teaspoon of this butter in each mushroom cap. Add remaining butter to the chopped mixture and mix all together. Stuff caps with this mixture and sprinkle with paprika. Put on broiler pan that has been preheated in a moderate oven (350°), or over charcoal fire on barbecue. Broil until done through, but no more; the caps should be on the solid side, not soft, when done. Serve hot. Makes 24 appetizers.

Irresistible: hot cheese balls filled with green or ripe olives—and they're good cold, too.

Olive-filled Cheese Balls

The bitiness of pimiento-stuffed green olives inside a coating of cheese makes these appetizers conversation pieces. They're good made with ripe olives, too.

1 cup (¼ lb.) shredded sharp Cheddar cheese
2 tablespoons butter
½ cup flour
Dash of cayenne
25 medium olives, well drained (pitted ripe or stuffed green)

Cream together cheese and butter. Blend in flour and cayenne. Wrap a teaspoonful of dough around each olive, covering completely. Bake in a hot oven (400°) for 15 minutes. Makes about 25 balls.

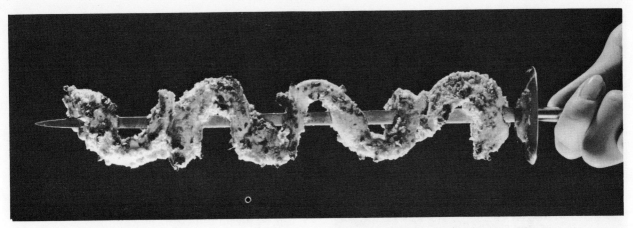

Sword skewer holds hot strips of Indonesian Broiled Chicken. Ground nut and lime juice marinade gives a crunchy coating. Chicken is served with special nut sauce.

Indonesian Broiled Chicken

This broiled chicken appetizer is an adaptation of a classic Indonesian entreé. You can do all the advance preparations early in the day and refrigerate the meat until it's time for you to cook the appetizers.

2 whole chicken breasts
1 package (8 oz.) chopped walnuts (2 cups)
⅔ cup lime juice
2 tablespoons chicken stock or broth
2 green onions, cut up
2 small cloves garlic, mashed
½ teaspoon salt
1 cup yogurt or sour cream

Cut uncooked chicken from bones in bite-size pieces and set aside. Combine nuts, lime juice, chicken stock, onions, garlic, and salt in an electric blender and whirl until the nuts are quite fine. Mix ½ cup of this nut mixture with the yogurt or sour cream to serve as a dip with the chicken; chill thoroughly.

Gently coat chicken pieces with remaining nut mixture and refrigerate for 2 to 3 hours. Then string the coated chicken pieces on skewers and refrigerate until you are ready to cook the meat. Broil or grill the chicken about 5 inches from heat for 5 to 7 minutes, turning once. Serve with the reserved sauce.

Appetizer Meat Balls

This recipe makes about 175 small bite-size meat balls. Mix and shape the balls well ahead of party time.

¾ cup soy sauce
¾ cup water
2 small cloves garlic, mashed
2 teaspoons ground ginger
3 pounds ground chuck or round steak

In a large bowl, combine the soy sauce, water, garlic, and ginger; mix until blended. Add the ground meat and blend lightly but thoroughly. Lift out spoonfuls of the meat mixture and lightly form with your hands into balls under 1 inch in diameter. If you plan to cook the meat balls later, cover with clear plastic film and refrigerate.

To cook the meat balls, arrange in a single layer in a large baking pan. Put into a slow oven (275°) and bake, uncovered, for about 15 minutes; turn once during the baking time. If you don't have a chafing dish or heated tray in which to serve these appetizers, turn your oven to lowest setting and keep part of the meat balls warm while serving the others. Serve with toothpicks. Makes about 175 appetizers.

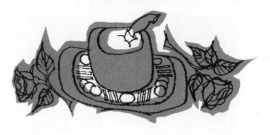

Chicken livers, water chestnuts, bacon, and soy sauce blend flavors in the Japanese appetizer, Rumaki.

Japanese Rumaki

You can prepare classic Japanese Rumaki ahead and refrigerate; then broil the appetizers in the kitchen, and keep them warm for serving on an electric tray or a covered dish.

¾ pound chicken livers, washed, drained, and cut in half
1 can (6½ oz.) whole water chestnuts, drained
½ pound bacon
½ cup soy sauce
1 small clove garlic, mashed
1 small dried, hot chili pepper, crushed
6 thin slices peeled, fresh ginger

Fold each piece of liver around a water chestnut, wrap with a half slice of bacon, and carefully fasten with wooden picks. Mix together the soy sauce, garlic, pepper, and ginger. Marinate the chicken liver bundles in this sauce for several hours, turning occasionally. Then place the appetizers on a rack in a shallow pan and broil for 5 to 7 minutes, turning once. Serve hot, along with hot Chinese mustard, if you wish. Makes about 18 appetizers.

Cream Cheese Turnovers

You can give variety to your hors d'oeuvre tray by using different fillings with one cream cheese pastry recipe. These turnovers are filled with smoked oysters, deviled ham, and Vienna sausage slices.

3 small packages (3 oz. each) pimiento cream cheese
½ cup (¼ lb.) butter or margarine
Dash of garlic powder
1 cup regular all-purpose flour

Fillings:
1 can (4½ oz.) deviled ham mixed with 2 tablespoons pickle relish
1 can (4 oz.) Vienna sausage with barbecue sauce
1 can (3⅔ oz.) tiny smoked oysters

Cream together cream cheese and butter; blend in garlic powder. Sift flour, measure, then gradually add to cheese mixture, mixing well. Shape into 2 balls and chill at least 2 hours.

On a well-floured board, roll out chilled pastry to ⅛-inch thickness; cut into 2-inch rounds with a biscuit cutter. On each round, spread one of the following: 1 teaspoon deviled ham and pickle mixture, a ½-inch slice of Vienna sausage topped with ¼ teaspoon barbecue sauce, or 1 small oyster. Fold over pastry rounds and crimp edges together with a fork. Place on a baking sheet and bake in moderate oven (350°) for 10 minutes, or until golden brown. Serve hot. Makes 100 small appetizers.

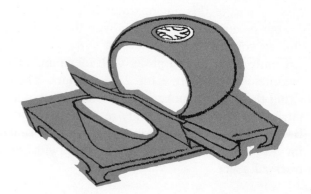

Guests can help themselves to Smoky Meat Balls, kept warm in a spicy tomato sauce in chafing dish.

Smoky Meat Balls

These meat balls simmer in a smoky barbecue sauce. Serve them from a chafing dish.

2 pounds lean ground beef
¼ cup chopped onion
1 teaspoon salt
¼ teaspoon pepper
¼ teaspoon garlic salt
½ cup fine cracker crumbs
1 egg
¼ cup milk
2 tablespoons salad oil
1 bottle (1 lb. 2 oz.) smoky-type barbecue sauce
1 cup water

Mix together until lightly blended the ground beef, onion, salt, pepper, garlic salt, cracker crumbs, egg, and milk. Shape into meat balls about the size of walnuts. Brown on all sides in hot salad oil. In a large pan, mix together until blended the barbecue sauce and water. Place the browned meat balls in this sauce and simmer for 15 minutes. Pour meat balls and sauce into a chafing dish, and serve with small picks. Makes about 8 dozen meat balls.

Turkey Meat Balls

If you have leftover turkey in your freezer, you can transform it into elegant hors d'oeuvres.

3 tablespoons butter or margarine
1 large onion, finely chopped
½ cup mashed potatoes
4 cups ground or very finely chopped cooked turkey meat
2 eggs, well beaten
1½ teaspoons salt
¼ teaspoon pepper
¼ teaspoon nutmeg
½ cup fine dry bread crumbs
2 tablespoons catsup
½ cup pickle relish
1 tablespoon minced parsley
1 clove garlic, minced or mashed
Butter or margarine for browning meat balls

In a large frying pan, heat the butter or margarine. Add the onion and mashed potato, and stir together until lightly browned. Add the turkey meat, eggs, salt, pepper, nutmeg, bread crumbs, catsup, pickle relish, parsley, and garlic; stir until well blended. Shape into small balls about the size of walnuts.

When you are ready to serve, brown turkey balls quickly in a small amount of butter or margarine. Transfer the browned turkey balls to a well-greased chafing dish and serve with toothpicks. Makes about 18 balls.

To broil on table top barbecue: beef, tomato, celery, green pepper; chicken, water chestnut, and mushroom.

Piping hot kebabs: bacon, pineapple, banana; chicken liver, bacon, mushroom; meat balls and banana.

AN IDEA FROM HAWAII

Colorful arrays of meat, fruit, and vegetables broiled and served on skewers have become so popular that they don't turn heads at a party. But make them in miniature on disposable bamboo sticks—just 3 or 4 tempting bits to each tiny kebab—and they'll capture your guests attention. These favorite recipes for tasty kebab combinations were collected in Hawaii, where hors d'oeuvres on skewers are popular party fare. You may serve the kebabs Hawaiian style—arranged ahead of time, with guests then broiling their own over a hibachi or other miniature barbecue. Or they can be broiled in the kitchen.

Skewers should be about 4 inches long. Bamboo sticks in 6 to 10-inch length can be purchased in Japanese stores; cut these and sharpen one end.

Cut foods so that each piece is bite-size. Use precooked foods when necessary so the kebab will broil in 3 to 5 minutes. Arrange foods on skewers with marinated meats between other foods to spread the juicy meat flavor; put firm bits on the ends to hold all the others in place.

Sauced before Broiling

Each of these skewered hors d'oeuvres is dipped or marinated in a sauce before broiling. Sauce recipes are given on the opposite page.

Chicken Liver, Bacon, Mushroom: Drop chicken livers into a mixture of hot butter and sherry (use 4 tablespoons butter and 2 tablespoons sherry for 1 pound of livers). Cook about 1 minute on each side; cool and cut into bite-size pieces. Partially cook strips of bacon; cut into 2-inch pieces. Use canned small whole mushrooms. Alternate on skewers, starting with mushrooms; fold each bacon piece. Dip in Teriyaki Sauce before broiling.

Beef, Tomato, Celery, Green Pepper: Use top sirloin or other good quality lean beef; slice very thin. Cut in 1-inch pieces. Marinate for 1½ to 2 hours in Teriyaki Sauce. Fold meat pieces to put on skewers between raw vegetables. Use small pieces of green pepper, celery, and tomato (halves of cherry tomatoes or quarters of small Italian tomatoes are best if you can get them). Dip in sauce; broil.

Chicken, Water Chestnuts, Mushrooms: Cut breasts of chicken or turkey into small squares. Marinate in Spicy Barbecue Sauce for about 1 hour, then sauté in a little butter or margarine to cook partially. Arrange on skewers with canned mushrooms and slices of canned water chestnuts, starting with mushrooms. Dip in sauce before broiling.

Shrimp, Mushroom, Green Pepper: Use small shrimp, shelled and deveined; drop into boiling water and simmer for 5 minutes. Marinate shrimp for about 1 hour in Spicy Barbecue Sauce. Arrange on skewers with small pieces of green pepper and canned whole or sliced mushrooms. Dip in sauce before broiling.

Pork, Apple, Pineapple: Use fully cooked fresh pork roast (leftover roast is fine). Cut into small squares, and marinate for about 1 hour in Teriyaki Sauce. Arrange on skewers with pineapple chunks and halved raw apple slices. Dip in sauce; broil. In place of pork, cubes of cooked duck or lamb roast are also delicious with pineapple and apple.

Frankfurter, Onion, Mushroom, Green Pepper: Cut frankfurters into small pieces; marinate in either Teriyaki Sauce or Spicy Barbecue Sauce for about 1 hour. Put on skewers with canned or precooked tiny white onions, canned mushrooms, and pieces of green pepper. Dip in sauce; broil.

Beef on a Stick: Cut top quality beef sirloin (raw) into tiny cubes. They may be marinated for ½ to 1 hour in Sesame Soy Sauce, or just put on the skewers and dip in the sauce before broiling.

Chicken or Turkey on a Stick: Cut raw chicken or turkey breasts into tiny cubes. Marinate in Sesame Soy Sauce, or dip into sauce before broiling. Broil until brown and tender, about 5 minutes.

Broiled Plain, Served with a Dunking Sauce

These are delicious broiled plain without any sauce. Simply provide several cold dunking sauces (recipes follow) in which your guests may dip the broiled appetizers if they wish.

Miniature Meat Balls: Use lean ground chuck or round, mix with egg, and season well; or use your favorite recipe for meat balls. Roll into tiny balls. Put 3 or 4 on each skewer or alternate meat with chunks of banana or pineapple; broil. Serve with Sour Cream-Onion Dip or Cheese Rabbit Dip.

Bacon, Pineapple, Banana: Partially cook bacon strips. Weave on skewers around chunks of canned pineapple and slices of banana; broil. Serve with Cheese Rabbit Dip.

Beef, Pineapple, Banana, Papaya: Use top sirloin or other good quality lean beef. Slice very thin and cut in 1-inch pieces. Fold pieces of beef and arrange on skewers between small chunks of banana, pineapple, and papaya (or mango); broil. Use Guacamole or no dip at all with these.

Chicken, Bacon, Avocado: Use chicken or turkey breasts or leftover roast turkey. Cut into small cubes. Brown uncooked poultry in a little butter until tender.

Partially cook bacon; cut firm avocado into chunks. Weave bacon skewer around chunks of chicken and avocado; broil. Serve with Guacamole Sauce.

The Sauce and Dips

The flavors of these sauces and dips combine especially well with the hors d'oeuvres described above, but you may want to try other combinations of your own. All of these are very easy to prepare.

Sesame Soy Sauce: Put 1 cup sesame seed into a dry frying pan; stir constantly over medium heat until seed is brown. Remove from heat. Combine sesame seed and 1 cup soy sauce, and whirl in a blender. (Or use a mortar and pestle and grind about ¼ cup of the seed at a time until it reaches the consistency of peanut butter, then add the soy sauce.) Add the following ingredients: 1 cup water, 1 crushed clove garlic, 1 tablespoon sugar, ½ cup vinegar, ½ cup sherry, 1 large apple finely grated. Let stand for at least 24 hours to blend flavors. Makes about 1 quart (leftover sauce keeps indefinitely).

Teriyaki Sauce: Combine 1 cup soy sauce, ½ cup sugar, 1 teaspoon monosodium glutamate, ¼ cup olive oil or salad oil, 2 teaspoons grated fresh ginger or 1 chopped clove garlic (optional), ½ cup sherry (optional). Stir until blended.

Spicy Barbecue Sauce: Use a prepared barbecue sauce or this Tomato Ginger Baste: Combine 1½ cups catsup, ¼ cup soy sauce, ⅓ cup brown sugar (firmly packed), 1 teaspoon salt, 1 teaspoon dry mustard, 1 clove garlic put through garlic press, and 2½ teaspoons ground ginger. Mix well, cover, and let stand for 2 hours to let flavors blend, or store in refrigerator until ready to use.

Cheese Rabbit Dip: Melt 2 tablespoons butter or margarine in top of a double boiler over direct heat. Stir in 2 tablespoons flour, ¾ teaspoon salt, ⅛ teaspoon pepper, ¼ teaspoon dry mustard; cook until bubbly. Gradually stir in 1½ cups milk and cook until thickened and smooth. Place over boiling water and stir in 2 cups shredded Cheddar cheese until melted and blended.

Sour Cream-Onion Dip: Blend a package of onion soup mix with 1 pint sour cream; let stand several hours so flavors blend.

Guacamole Dip: Mash 2 large avocados with 1 large tomato (peeled, chopped, and drained). Add 1 small onion, chopped fine, 1 tablespoon wine vinegar, salt, pepper, and chopped green chili peppers to taste; mix well.

Ham and Cheese Custard Squares

Instead of baking this version of "Quiche Lorraine" in a pie pan as in the original recipe, you put it into a pastry-lined shallow pan. When it is baked you cut it in bite-size squares.

Pastry for two 9-inch pie shells
2 tablespoons flour
¾ cup finely diced baked or boiled ham
1 cup finely shredded Swiss cheese
2 whole eggs
2 egg yolks
1 cup milk
1 cup light cream
½ teaspoon dry mustard
½ teaspoon salt
⅛ teaspoon pepper
Dash nutmeg
1 teaspoon Worcestershire

Line a 10 by 15-inch jelly roll pan with pastry, making a fluted edge about ¾ inch high. Sprinkle flour over bottom of crust. Arrange ham in a layer; cover with a layer of cheese. Beat eggs and yolks with a fork; add milk, cream, and seasonings. Pour into pastry-lined pan. Bake in a moderate oven (350°) for 45 to 50 minutes, or until filling is set and crust is lightly browned. Serve hot, cut in 1½-inch squares.

To make ahead, line the pan with pastry, add the ham and cheese layers, cover with clear plastic film, and store in refrigerator. Prepare the egg mixture, cover, and refrigerate. About 55 to 60 minutes before serving, pour egg mixture over ham and cheese and bake. Makes about 80.

Chinese Barbecued Pork (below) and Oyster Beef Appetizers (page 17) alternate on grill. Guests can cook their own skewered appetizers.

Chinese Barbecued Pork

Cinnamon, cloves, and anise flavor the pork for these hot appetizers.

¼ cup soy sauce
2 tablespoons salad oil
2 cloves garlic, mashed
1 small dried, hot chili pepper, crushed
½ teaspoon sugar
¼ teaspoon anise seed
⅛ teaspoon cinnamon
⅛ teaspoon cloves
1 pound lean pork, cut into bite-size strips or cubes
1 small fresh pineapple
1 medium-sized green pepper

Combine the soy sauce, salad oil, garlic, pepper, sugar, anise, cinnamon, and cloves in a bowl. Add the pork and stir gently to coat each piece with the marinade. Refrigerate meat 1 to 2 hours, stirring occasionally. String pork on skewers with bite-sized pieces of fresh pineapple and green pepper. Broil or grill about 5 inches from the source of heat for 7 to 10 minutes, turning once. Serve hot.

Parsley Meat Balls

These bite-size meat balls are seasoned wth parsley, mint, and onion, and then sprinkled with wine vinegar and oregano.

¾ cup fine dry bread crumbs
½ cup milk
2 onions, chopped
½ cup water
2 pounds ground chuck
¾ cup finely chopped parsley
3 leaves mint, chopped
2 egg yolks
3 small cloves garlic, minced or mashed
1½ teaspoons salt
¼ teaspoon pepper
1½ tablespoons olive oil
1½ tablespoons butter
¼ cup (4 tablespoons) red wine vinegar or
    lemon juice
½ teaspoon crumbled dried oregano

Soak bread crumbs in milk; then beat up until mushy. Cook onions, covered, in the water until the water has boiled away. Mix together thoroughly the meat, soaked bread crumbs, cooked onions, parsley, mint, egg yolks, garlic, salt, and pepper. Form into walnut-shaped balls. Heat the oil and butter, and brown meat balls on all sides, slowly and well. Transfer meat balls to a serving dish. Pour wine vinegar into the pan, heat, and scrape up the drippings; pour over the meat balls. Sprinkle with oregano. Makes 3 dozen meat balls.

Oyster Beef Appetizers

Oyster sauce (bottled like soy sauce) is a necessary ingredient for this hot appetizer. The sauce may be purchased in most Oriental markets.

¼ cup oyster sauce
2 tablespoons salad oil
2 tablespoons soy sauce
1 clove garlic, mashed
2 green onions, chopped
¼ teaspoon sugar
1 pound beef sirloin, cut into bite-size strips or
    cubes
½ pound fresh mushrooms, washed and drained
1 can (6½ oz.) whole water chestnuts, drained
3 green onions, cut into 1-inch pieces

Combine the oyster sauce, salad oil, soy sauce, garlic, chopped onion, and sugar in a bowl. Marinate the beef and mushrooms in this mixture for 1 to 2 hours in the refrigerator. Then string meat, mushrooms, water chestnuts, and pieces of green onion on skewers. Broil or grill about 5 inches from source of heat for 5 minutes, turning once.

Bacon-banded Olives

This is a nice change from the more familiar appetizer of stuffed green olives wrapped in bacon strips.

Sliced bacon
Finely minced onion
1 large can (7½ oz.) pitted ripe olives,
    well drained

Cut each slice of bacon in half lengthwise, then cut each strip crosswise into thirds. Stuff minced onion into the cavity of each olive, wrap with a piece of bacon, and fasten with a toothpick. Arrange stuffed and wrapped olives on a cooky sheet, leaving 1 inch between each one. When ready to serve, heat olives under the broiler or in a very hot oven (450°) until bacon is crisp. If you broil them, turn olives once during cooking.

Anchovy Turnovers

Serve these flaky tiny turnovers while still hot. You make them ahead, refrigerate, and bake just before serving.

1 small package (3 oz.) cream cheese, softened
½ cup (¼ lb.) butter, softened
1 cup regular, all purpose flour
1 tube (2 oz.) anchovy paste

Cream together cheese and butter; sift flour, measure, and add gradually to the butter mixture, mixing until a smooth dough forms. Chill. Turn out onto a lightly floured board, roll out to about ¼-inch thickness, and cut into rounds 1½ to 2 inches in diameter. Place about ¼ teaspoon anchovy paste in the center of each round, moisten edges, and press together to make a turnover. Chill until serving time. Bake in a moderately hot oven (375°) for 10 minutes; serve. Makes 4 dozen appetizers.

Chicken Almond Puffs

All the chicken flavor is baked into these crisp little cream puff appetizers. You save the time usually spent splitting and filling cocktail puffs.

1 cup flour
¼ teaspoon salt
½ cup (¼ lb.) butter or margarine
1 cup chicken stock or broth
4 eggs
½ cup finely diced cooked chicken
2 tablespoons chopped toasted almonds
Few grains paprika

Sift the flour, measure, and sift again with the salt. Combine the butter and chicken stock in a pan; keep over low heat until the butter is melted. Add the flour all at once and stir vigorously over low heat until the mixture forms a ball and leaves the sides of the pan. Remove from the heat. Add the eggs, one at a time, and beat thoroughly after each one is added. Continue beating until a thick dough is formed. Stir in the chicken, almonds, and paprika. Drop by small teaspoonfuls onto a greased baking sheet. Bake in a very hot oven (450°) for 10 minutes. Reduce heat to 350°, and bake for 5 to 10 minutes longer or until browned. Makes 4 to 5 dozen appetizers.

Korean Style Beef Cubes

Few can resist these spicy beef cubes, sprinkled with soy sauce and special black sesame seed. Cooked quickly, they are brown on the outside and rare inside.

¼ cup soy sauce
3 tablespoons sliced fresh ginger
4 cloves garlic, sliced (about 3 teaspoons)
1½ teaspoons sugar
Tops of 3 green onions, sliced
4 small hot red chilies, seeded and crushed
1½ pounds boneless beef sirloin, or high quality top round, cut in ¾-inch cubes
2 tablespoons salad oil
1½ tablespoons soy sauce
1 tablespoon chopped black sesame seed, toasted, or standard sesame seed, toasted

To make the marinade for the beef, combine the ¼ cup soy sauce, ginger, garlic, sugar, onions, and chilies. About 30 minutes before you plan to serve, stir beef cubes into the marinade; let stand for ½ hour, stirring once or twice.

To serve, heat salad oil in an electric frying pan. Add the drained meat cubes and cook, stirring, to brown all sides, for about 2 minutes, or until done the way you like it. Turn out on a warm plate; sprinkle with soy sauce, then with sesame seed. Makes about 4 dozen appetizers.

Four flavor variations are baked into these tasty Hungarian Cocktail Sticks. They can be reheated.

Hungarian Cocktail Sticks

These cocktail sticks have crisp crusts and rich, tender centers. You can make four spicy flavor variations all in one baking.

1 cup warmed mashed potatoes
1 cup flour
½ cup (¼ lb.) butter
½ teaspoon salt
1 egg yolk, slightly beaten
1 tablespoon milk
4 tablespoons sesame seed
2 teaspoons caraway seed
3 tablespoons grated Parmesan cheese

In a bowl, mix together potatoes, flour, butter, and salt to form a smooth dough. Shape into a ball on a floured board; roll out to a ¼-inch thickness. Paint dough with slightly beaten egg yolk thinned with milk. Cut dough into quarters; sprinkle two sections with sesame seed and two sections with caraway seed. Then sprinkle one sesame section and one caraway section with grated Parmesan cheese. Cut into sticks ½ inch

wide and 3 inches long. Bake now or refrigerate to bake later. To bake, place on greased cooky sheet. Bake in moderately hot oven (375°) about 12 minutes. Makes 4 dozen appetizers.

Bacon-wrapped Stuffed Prunes and Dates

You can cook a whole artichoke for these unusual appetizers—the heart is used in the stuffing for the fruits, and the leaves are used as tiny servers. If you prefer, you can substitute a pickled artichoke heart for the stuffing and omit the leaf servers.

12 large prunes, pitted
1 slice lemon
12 large dates, pitted
½ cup finely chopped celery
1 cooked artichoke heart, finely chopped
1 package (3 oz.) cream cheese
Juice of ½ lemon
Dash of cayenne
¼ teaspoon salt
12 slices bacon

Soak prunes overnight in water with a slice of lemon. (Do not soak dates.) Drain prunes. To make the filling, combine celery, artichoke heart, cream cheese, lemon juice, cayenne, and salt. Stuff prunes and dates with this mixture. Cut bacon slices in half, and wrap a slice around each prune and each date; fasten ends with a cocktail pick. Grill for 4 to 5 minutes on each side until bacon is crisp. If you cooked a fresh artichoke, save the leaves and arrange on a platter. Serve each prune and date on an artichoke leaf. Makes 24 appetizers.

Spicy Grilled Shrimp

Cook these shrimp appetizers on your grill before a guest barbecue meal. If you prefer not to use your barbecue, cook the meat in your broiler.

1 teaspoon chili powder
1 tablespoon vinegar
¼ teaspoon pepper
1 clove garlic, minced or mashed
1 teaspoon salt
1 teaspoon basil
1 tablespoon finely chopped fresh mint
¾ cup salad oil
2 pounds medium-sized shrimp or prawns, washed, shelled, and deveined, or about 1½ pounds frozen deveined large shrimp (they need not be thawed)

In a bowl or glass jar, blend the chili powder with the vinegar, pepper, garlic, salt, basil, and mint. Stir in the oil and shake or mix until well blended. Pour over the shrimp, cover the dish, and marinate in the refrigerator for at least 4 hours, or overnight. Thread the shrimp on skewers and grill for 6 to 10 minutes (depending on size), turning once and basting liberally with the marinade. If you cook the shrimp in your broiler, they need not be strung on skewers. Arrange them on your broiler rack, and broil, turning once and basting well; time will be about the same. Makes 50 appetizers.

Banana Chip Appetizers

Thinly slice green-tipped, peeled bananas. Coat slices lightly with flour. Fry in deep fat heated to 375° for about 3 minutes or until golden brown. Drain on paper towels, sprinkle with salt or prepared cinnamon sugar, and serve hot.

Prawns alla Rimini

These elegant hot appetizers were inspired by the way large shrimp (scampi) are prepared in the old seacoast town of Rimini, Italy. You can make them ahead and broil just before serving.

2 tablespoons olive oil or salad oil
1 tablespoon lemon juice
2 tablespoons water
½ cup fine dry bread crumbs
2 teaspoons garlic salt
Dash pepper
2 teaspoons chopped fresh or dried parsley
1 pound fresh prawns or large shrimp (about 30), shelled, deveined, and dried well

In a small bowl combine the olive oil, lemon juice, and water. In another bowl or on a piece of waxed paper, mix together the bread crumbs, garlic salt, pepper, and parsley. Dip each prawn first in the oil mixture, then roll in the bread crumb mixture to coat all over. Arrange the breaded prawns in a single layer on a foil-lined cooky sheet. Cover and refrigerate, if you plan to broil them later.

Just before serving, set the pan of prawns into a pre-heated broiler, about 4 inches from the heat. Broil about 3 minutes; turn them carefully with a spatula and broil about 3 minutes on the other side, or until lightly browned. Serve with picks for your guests to help themselves. Makes about 30 appetizers.

Peanut Butter and Bacon Rollups

Peanut butter, bacon, and pumpernickel bread are a tasty blend in these simple hors d'oeuvres.

8 thin slices pumpernickel bread, crusts removed
½ to ¾ cup peanut butter
8 slices bacon, cut in half crosswise and
    lengthwise

Roll pumpernickel slices with rolling pin to prevent their cracking. Spread with smooth peanut butter and cut each slice into 4 strips. Roll up peanut butter strips, wrap bacon around them, fasten with toothpick. Refrigerate until ready to broil. Cook bacon on all sides. Makes 32.

Serve piping hot Peanut Butter and Bacon Rollups for an easy appetizer that will delight guests.

Mushrooms Provençale

This appetizer is made by stuffing mushroom caps with a mixture of the mushroom stems, chives, and anchovies.

1 pound mushrooms, each about 1¼ inches
    in diameter
¼ cup olive oil
2 cloves garlic, crushed
¼ cup minced chives
½ cup fine dry bread crumbs
1 can (2 oz.) anchovy fillets, drained
    and chopped

Cook mushrooms in olive oil, along with garlic, for 4 minutes. Cool and remove stems. Reserve caps. Chop stems and mix with chives, bread crumbs, anchovies, and the juices left in the sauté pan. Stuff mushroom caps with the mixture. Just before serving, slip the pan of stuffed mushrooms under the broiler to heat and brown slightly.

Cherry Tomatoes and Shrimps in Herb Butter

Why not prepare this appetizer from start to finish right before your guests? All you do is simmer the shrimps in an herb butter, add the tomatoes and heat.

½ cup (¼ pound) butter
⅛ teaspoon curry powder
½ teaspoon basil
¼ teaspoon celery seed
¼ teaspoon salt
Freshly ground pepper
1 pound medium-sized shrimp (about 40),
    shelled and deveined
1 cup firm ripe cherry tomatoes, stems removed
15 small tart shells (optional)

Melt butter in chafing dish; add seasonings. When simmering, add shrimp and stir and cook until shellfish are bright pink (about 5 minutes). Add tomatoes; baste with butter until heated through. Keep warm over low flame. To serve, spear shrimp and tomato with cocktail picks. Or spoon a few shrimp, a tomato, and some of the butter into a tart for each serving. Makes about 15 appetizers.

Cheese Straws

These crisp little strips of cheese pastry make elegant party hors d'oeuvres.

1 cup regular all-purpose flour
½ teaspoon salt
½ teaspoon monosodium glutamate
½ teaspoon powdered ginger
⅓ cup shortening (may be part butter)
1 cup (¼ lb.) shredded sharp process cheese
¼ cup sesame seed, toasted
½ teaspoon Worcestershire
2 to 2½ tablespoons cold water

Sift flour, measure, and sift with salt, monosodium glutamate, and ginger. Cut in shortening with a pastry blender as you would for pastry. Lightly stir in cheese and sesame seeds. Add Worcestershire to 1 tablespoon of the water, sprinkle over flour, and toss with a fork. Add remaining water while tossing mixture with a fork until moistened. Gather up with fingers and form into a ball. On a lightly floured board, roll out ⅛ inch thick. Cut with a pastry wheel or knife into strips about 3 inches long and ½ inch wide. To freeze, put into your freezer unbaked; do not thaw out before baking. To bake, place on ungreased baking sheet in a hot oven (400°) for 10 to 12 minutes, or until lightly browned and crisp. Makes 6 to 7 dozen appetizers.

Shrimp and Bacon Bits

Freshly cooked shrimp, seasoned and wrapped in bacon, make delicious party tidbits. You can get these ready early and refrigerate them until it is time to broil and serve.

1 pound medium-large shrimp or prawns
Boiling salted water
About ½ pound thinly sliced bacon
1 clove garlic, minced or mashed
½ cup chili sauce

Starting several hours before you plan to serve these, cook the shrimp in the boiling salted water until they turn pink, about 5 minutes. Drain and cool enough to shell and devein them. Also broil bacon slices on one side only (they should not be crisp); drain, and cut each slice in half crosswise. Blend the garlic into the chili sauce. Dip each shrimp into the sauce to coat all over, wrap in the half slice of bacon, and secure with a toothpick. When all are prepared, cover and refrigerate until you are ready to broil and serve them.

Arrange the appetizers on a broiler rack and broil until they are heated through and the bacon is crisp; turn to brown and crisp both sides. Serve hot. Makes about 2 dozen appetizers.

Onion and Anchovy Strips

Serve these appetizers piping hot.

4 medium-sized onions, thinly sliced
2 tablespoons olive oil or salad oil
3 tablespoons heavy cream
¼ teaspoon pepper
½ teaspoon nutmeg
⅛ teaspoon cayenne pepper
1-pound loaf unsliced white bread
4 tablespoons olive oil or soft butter
2 cans (2 oz. each) anchovy fillets
2½ tablespoons grated Parmesan cheese

Cook onions in the 2 tablespoons olive oil slowly and without browning for 10 minutes. Add cream, pepper, nutmeg, and cayenne; cover and continue cooking, stirring often, until very soft, about 15 minutes. Meanwhile cut the crusts from loaf of bread; cut loaf lengthwise into 4 long slices. Arrange bread slices on an ungreased cooky sheet and brush with the 4 tablespoons olive oil or butter; put under broiler until lightly browned. Spread with the hot onion mixture and arrange about 6 anchovy fillets across each bread slice. Sprinkle with cheese and put into a moderately hot oven (375°) for about 10 minutes, or until piping hot. Cut each bread slice crosswise into 6 strips. Makes 24 appetizers.

Chinese Meat Balls

These tiny meat balls are fried in deep fat before the party, then simmered in a flavorful glaze in a chafing dish.

2 cans (20 oz. each) water chestnuts
3 bunches green onions
5 pounds lean pork, ground
¼ cup soy sauce
6 eggs, slightly beaten
1 tablespoon salt
2½ cups fine dry bread crumbs
Cornstarch
Fat for deep frying

Drain and chop water chestnuts; chop green onions, tops and all; mix both with meat. Add soy sauce, eggs, salt, and bread crumbs; mix thoroughly with your hands. Chill. Form into balls, using a rounded teaspoon for each; roll lightly in cornstarch. Fry in deep fat at 370° until well browned.

Sauce:
1 cup vinegar
2 cups pineapple juice
¾ cup sugar
2 cups canned consommé
2 tablespoons soy sauce
3 tablespoons grated fresh ginger, or 5 tablespoons chopped crystallized ginger
½ cup cornstarch
1 cup cold water

Heat together vinegar, pineapple juice, sugar, consommé, soy sauce, and ginger. Gradually stir in cornstarch mixed with cold water. Cook, stirring, until clear and thickened. Keep meat balls hot in chafing dish with just enough sauce to form a slight glaze.

Freezer Cheese Sticks

A little effort with a loaf of frozen bread can reward you with a good supply of snacks, ready to toast in the oven any time you want them.

1 large loaf white sandwich bread, unsliced
½ cup (¼ pound) butter or margarine
1 container (5 oz.) pasteurized process
    sharp cheese spread
1 egg white

Put the loaf of bread in the freezer until frozen solid. Have the butter and the cheese spread at room temperature when you begin.

While the bread is still frozen, trim off crusts. With a long, sharp knife, cut into 3 lengthwise slices, then make crosswise cuts about ¾ inch apart. Beat the egg white slightly; add the softened butter and the cheese spread, and beat until well blended and smooth. Spread on all sides of the cheese sticks. Arrange on greased cooky sheets about 1 inch apart, and cover with clear plastic film. Keep in freezer until you are ready to bake them. Bake the frozen sticks in a moderately slow oven (325°) for 15 to 20 minutes, or until lightly browned. Serve piping hot. Makes about 4 dozen cheese sticks.

Imperial Crab

Tiny balls of crab meat make these delicious party appetizers.

1 egg
1 pound fresh crab meat, or 2 cans (6½ oz. ea.)
    crab meat
1 cup mayonnaise
½ teaspoon dry mustard
½ green pepper, chopped
1 cup unsalted cracker crumbs

Beat the egg well. Add crab meat, mayonnaise, mustard, and green pepper. Shape into small balls and roll in cracker crumbs. Fry in deep fat at 350° for about 6 minutes, or until golden brown. Makes enough appetizers for about 20 people.

Cucumber rolls (left) and Steamed Egg Roll (right) are Japanese specialties that make delicious appetizers. Serve Cucumber Rolls on thin crackers or small toast rounds; slice Egg Roll and serve as finger food. Recipes on pages 30 and 34.

COLD APPETIZERS
Savory morsels to tempt your guests

Brazil Nut Chips

Serve these as a snack with beverages. They are irresistible.

1 pound shelled Brazil nuts
Boiling water
3 tablespoons butter
About 1 teaspoon salt

Cover Brazil nuts with boiling water and boil for 7 minutes. Drain, scrape off brown skin (it will come off easily), then cut lengthwise in thin slices. Spread out in a shallow pan and dot with butter. Put in a moderate oven (350°) and bake until lightly browned (12 to 15 minutes), stirring occasionally. Drain on paper towels, then sprinkle lightly with salt. Serve as you would salted nuts.

Curry or Chili Cheese Logs

You can season these cheese nut rolls with either curry or chili powder. Try one roll of each.

1 large package (8 oz.) cream cheese
½ pound sharp Cheddar cheese, finely shredded
2 cloves garlic, minced or mashed
1 cup finely chopped pecans or walnuts
2 tablespoons curry powder or chili powder

Cream together the cheeses and garlic until blended; mix in chopped nuts. Shape into 2 rolls, each about 1½ inches in diameter. Roll in curry or chili powder which you've sprinkled on waxed paper. Wrap each roll in waxed paper or in clear plastic film and chill. Slice into rounds ⅛ inch thick and serve with thin crisp crackers. Makes about 150 appetizers.

Sesame Seed Cocktailers

These extra-short pastries are full of toasted sesame seed. To keep them crisp for storing, pack in a waxed-paper-lined can with a tight-fitting cover.

1 cup sesame seed
2¼ cups regular all-purpose flour
1 teaspoon salt
Dash of cayenne
¾ cup butter or margarine
3 to 4 tablespoons cold water
Salt (optional)

Toast sesame seed by sprinkling on baking sheet. Place in hot oven (400°), stirring occasionally, until lightly browned. (Or heat, stirring, in heavy frying pan until light brown.) Sift flour, measure, and sift again into mixing bowl with the 1 teaspoon salt and cayenne. With pastry blender or two knives, cut in butter until the size of small peas. Toss in water to make dough of pie-crust consistency. Mix in toasted seed. On a lightly floured board, roll out dough very thin (about ⅛ inch thick). Cut into small sticks, rounds, or other shapes. Place on ungreased baking sheet. Bake in slow oven (300°) for 35 minutes or until golden brown. Sprinkle very lightly with more salt, if you wish. Remove to cooling racks. Makes 6 dozen appetizers.

Caviar with Deviled Eggs

For a party or a fancy picnic appetizer, try stuffed eggs topped with caviar.

5 hard-cooked eggs
2 teaspoons lemon juice
2½ tablespoons mayonnaise or sour cream
Salt and pepper
About 2½ teaspoons caviar

Cut eggs in half lengthwise and remove yolks. Mash yolks to a fine paste with lemon juice, mayonnaise or sour cream, and salt and pepper to taste. Pipe or spoon the yolk mixture into the egg whites, leaving a small depression in the center of each; fill each hollow with about ¼ teaspoon caviar. Makes 10 appetizers.

Stuffed Mushroom Caps

A mixture of liverwurst, cream cheese, and anchovies is used to stuff these mushroom caps.

1 pound uniform-sized mushrooms
3 tablespoons butter
¼ pound liverwurst
1 small package (3 oz.) cream cheese
½ teaspoon salt
2 teaspoons lemon juice
2 anchovy fillets, finely chopped
Finely minced chives or parsley, or grated toasted almonds

Remove mushroom stems; put caps and stems and butter in a covered pan. Cook over very low heat for 10 minutes. Remove caps; save stems and juice for soup or sauce. Mash liverwurst and mix with cream cheese, salt, lemon juice, and anchovies. Stuff mushroom caps with cheese mixture; sprinkle with chives, parsley, or almonds. Serve cold. Makes enough filling for 24 mushroom caps about 1½ inches in diameter.

Pickled Onion Appetizers

This appetizer is easy to make up ahead of time. The pickled onion filling provides plenty of seasoning.

2 small packages (3 oz. each) cream cheese
24 pickled onions
Finely chopped watercress, chopped parsley, or ground dried beef

Cut each cake of cream cheese into 12 squares (easy to do with a piece of string, or a butter wrapper over a knife); let stand at room temperature until soft. Roll each square of cheese into a ball; press a hole in the center, and stuff with a well-drained pickled onion; close hole and reshape cheese into a ball. Roll stuffed balls in watercress, parsley, or dried beef until well coated. Chill in refrigerator for at least 1 hour. Provide toothpicks to spear the balls. Makes 24 appetizers.

Cheddar Chive Crisps

Slice and bake these cheese-rich rounds as you would refrigerator cookies. They are good served either hot or cold.

½ pound (about 2 cups) shredded Cheddar cheese
½ cup (¼ lb.) soft butter or margarine
½ teaspoon salt
Dash of cayenne
2 tablespoons finely chopped chives
1½ cups regular all-purpose flour

Combine cheese with butter, salt, cayenne, and chives. Sift flour, measure, and add to cheese. Mix until a smooth dough forms. Divide dough in half, and shape each into a log about 1 inch in diameter. Wrap in waxed paper and chill. Slice into ⅛-inch slices and bake on a lightly greased cooky sheet in a moderate oven (350°) for 10 minutes or until lightly browned. Makes about 48 appetizers.

Avocado Appetizers

These hors d'oeuvres are made by dipping avocado cubes in a mayonnaise-anchovy paste mixture and then rolling them in toasted almonds.

1 large avocado, ripe but firm
¼ cup mayonnaise
2 teaspoons anchovy paste
1 teaspoon lemon juice
About 1 teaspoon milk or water
⅔ cup almonds, chopped coarsely

Cut avocado in half, remove skin, and cut in 24 to 30 pieces, making them as nearly cubes as possible. Mix together mayonnaise, anchovy paste, lemon juice, and a little milk or water to thin. Spread almonds on a baking sheet, and toast in a moderate oven (350°) for 8 to 10 minutes, or until lightly browned. (Watch carefully, as the nuts can go from golden to black in a matter of seconds.)

Dip the avocado pieces in the mayonnaise mixture, then roll in the chopped toasted almonds. Serve on cocktail picks. Makes 24 to 30 appetizers.

Cheese-stuffed Dates

You make this appetizer by stuffing dates with sharply seasoned cream cheese and then rolling them in a mixture of paprika and finely ground nut meats.

1 small package (3 oz.) cream cheese
1 teaspoon finely minced chives
1 teaspoon finely minced green pepper
1 tablespoon pickle relish
1 tablespoon mayonnaise
Dash of liquid hot-pepper seasoning
Salt and pepper to taste
½ pound dates (about 25 dates), pitted
½ cup finely ground nut meats
1 teaspoon paprika

Whip together cream cheese, chives, green pepper, pickle relish, mayonnaise, liquid hot-pepper seasoning, salt and pepper. Stuff into pitted dates. Roll in nut meats mixed with paprika. Store in refrigerator until serving time. Makes about 25 appetizers.

Artichoke Appetizers

Each artichoke leaf is a container for a tasty morsel of cheese and shrimp when you serve these hors d'oeuvres. You can arrange the leaves on your tray to resemble a flower.

1 large artichoke
Water
1 teaspoon salad oil
1 bay leaf, crushed
½ teaspoon salt
1 package (3 oz.) cream cheese
¼ teaspoon liquid hot-pepper seasoning
½ teaspoon garlic powder
About 2 tablespoons cream
About ¼ pound small shrimp
Paprika

In a tightly covered container cook the artichoke in water to cover; add the oil, bay leaf, and salt to the cooking water. Simmer for about 30 minutes, or until tender; cool, then remove the leaves. Use the leaves that are firm enough to handle and have a good edible portion on the ends. Blend the cream cheese with hot-pepper seasoning, garlic powder, additional salt to taste, and cream to make a smooth paste. Spread this filling on the tip of each leaf. Place a small shrimp on top of the filling and sprinkle with paprika. Arrange on a round plate or tray in the shape of a sunflower so each leaf is easy to pick up. Makes about 18 appetizers.

Cherry Tomatoes with Smoked Oysters

Fresh tomatoes and smoked oysters are an unusual flavor combination in these attractive, easy-to-make appetizers.

About 40 cherry tomatoes
1 can (3 oz.) tiny smoked oysters

Cut down through each tomato to within about ¼ inch of the base; spread apart and slip a canned smoked oyster inside each one. Makes about 40 appetizers.

To savor before dinner: deviled eggs with almonds, salmon cheese rolls, stuffed celery, cherry tomatoes with oysters, salami with pickle slices.

Salmon-Cream Cheese Rolls

The delicate colors of salmon, cream cheese, and fresh parsley make these hors d'oeuvres attractive additions to your tray.

¾ pound thinly sliced, lightly smoked salmon (called lox)
2 small packages (3 oz. each) cream cheese
2 tablespoons light cream
¼ teaspoon onion salt
½ teaspoon dill weed
Fresh parsley, cut in tiny sprigs

Cut each slice of salmon into pieces about 2 or 2½ inches square. Blend together cream cheese, cream, onion salt, and dill weed. Spread each piece of the salmon thinly, but completely, with the cheese. Roll each into the shape of a log. Arrange on the tray with cut sides down and garnish with parsley sprigs tucked into the ends. Makes 18 appetizers.

Deviled Eggs with Salted Almonds

Deviled eggs are ever-popular hors d'oeuvres. Your guests will savor this version, sprinkled with salted almonds.

9 hard-cooked eggs
3 tablespoons mayonnaise
3 tablespoons sour cream
1 teaspoon salt
2 teaspoons Swedish or Russian-style mustard
¼ cup chopped salted almonds

Halve the hard-cooked eggs and scoop out the yolks. Mash yolks with mayonnaise, sour cream, salt, and mustard. Press this mixture through a pastry tube with a star-shaped tip, or use a spoon to fill the whites. Sprinkle almonds over the centers. Makes 18 appetizers.

Pickle-Salami Cornucopias

You simply wrap pickle with salami to make this tasty appetizer.

For each appetizer, place a bread-and-butter pickle slice on a thin slice of salami; fold salami over the pickle into a cornucopia shape and secure with a toothpick.

Stuffed Kumquats and Litchi Nuts

The flavors of fruit and cheese are combined in these elegant, colorful appetizers.

1 large package (8 oz.) cream cheese
⅛ teaspoon salt
1 tablespoon sherry
3 tablespoons chopped nuts (walnuts, pecans, macadamias)
1 can (1 lb., 4 oz.) litchi nuts, drained
1 jar (15½ oz.) preserved whole kumquats (or about 25 fresh kumquats)

Place cream cheese in bowl; add salt, sherry, and nuts, creaming together well. You can do this the day before.

Stuff each litchi nut with about 1 teaspoon filling. With a sharp knife, cut kumquats in half, remove seeds, and sandwich the halves together after placing about 1 teaspoon of filling mixture in each one. Makes about 50 appetizers.

Oaxacan Peanuts

Cacahuetes, as they are called in Oaxaca, are wonderful nibbling. They are flavored with dried red chilies called *serrano*. These nuts improve with standing, especially if stirred occasionally.

20 small dried red chilies
4 cloves garlic, crushed
2 tablespoons olive oil
2 pounds blanched salted Virginia peanuts (canned peanuts are very reliable)
1 teaspoon Kosher salt or coarse salt from salt mill
1 teaspoon chili powder

Heat chilies and garlic in olive oil for 1 minute. Stir so the chilies won't scorch. Mash garlic well (or put through a press, if you prefer). Mix in peanuts and stir in a heavy pan over medium heat, or spread on a cooky sheet and bake in a moderate oven (350°) for 5 minutes, or until slightly brown. Sprinkle with coarse salt and chili powder. Mix well and store in a covered jar or tin.

These are conversation pieces: stuffed kumquats with a savory nut and cheese filling flavored with sherry.

Curried Almonds

These simple appetizers are all you need to serve if the meal is to follow shortly.

2 pounds almonds, blanched or unblanched
¼ cup salad oil
2 tablespoons fresh curry powder
Salt

To dry and crisp recently blanched almonds, spread them in a pan and bake in a slow oven (300°) for 20 or 30 minutes.

Heat salad oil in large frying pan. Add almonds; sprinkle them with fresh curry powder. Sauté, stirring, until nicely colored. Sprinkle with salt and drain on paper towels. Serve hot or cold.

Cucumber Rolls

Cucumber rolls are a Japanese specialty. Serve them on thin crackers or small toast rounds.

2 large cucumbers, peeled (discard ends)
1 quart water
1 tablespoon salt
1 cup (½ lb.) crab meat
4 hard-cooked egg yolks
2 tablespoons mayonnaise
1 teaspoon salt

Cut two 2½ to 3-inch lengths from each cucumber. Put into water with the 1 tablespoon salt; let stand about 20 minutes. Holding each cucumber piece upright and using sharp knife, cut ⅛ inch around full length spirally to center (see photo); discard centers. Dry well. Open out the spiral and spread a mixture of the crab meat, egg yolks, mayonnaise, and the 1 teaspoon salt inside cucumber. Reroll from center to outside. Chill for about 1 hour. Slice ½ inch thick. Makes about 20 appetizers.

To make Cucumber Rolls, cut cucumber section spirally to center, then open out flat and spread with filling; reroll and chill thoroughly; slice to serve.

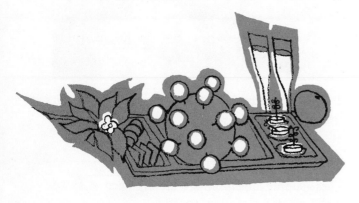

Turkey Cubes

This appetizer is easily made from leftover turkey.

White or dark turkey meat (thawed if frozen)
1 cup mayonnaise
1 teaspoon soy
1 tablespoon grated green or candied ginger, or
    2 teaspoons curry powder
Chopped, toasted blanched almonds

Cut turkey in neat cubes. Mix mayonnaise with soy and ginger or curry powder. Roll the turkey cubes in this mixture, covering them on all sides; then roll in almonds. Impale on wooden picks and chill until serving time.

Savory Meat Sticks

By varying the coatings, you make four different appetizers from this basic meat stick recipe.

1 teaspoon dried tarragon, crumbled
1 tablespoon lemon juice
1 teaspoon gelatin
2 tablespoons cold water
1 cup mayonnaise
Cooked turkey, ham, or roast beef, cut in sticks
    ½ inch square and 3 inches long
Finely chopped almonds, minced green onions,
    chopped parsley, and toasted sesame seed

Soak tarragon in lemon juice for 15 minutes. Soften gelatin in cold water. Stir tarragon-lemon juice mixture into mayonnaise. Melt gelatin over boiling water and stir into mayonnaise; mix well. Dip turkey, ham, or meat sticks into mayonnaise, leaving 1 inch undipped at the end for a handle; roll sticks in chopped nuts, or in one of the other coatings, and chill well before serving.

Marinated Raw Mushrooms

Try two different ways to flavor this interesting appetizer, one with tarragon and one with anchovies.

1 pound uniform mushrooms
¾ cup olive oil
3 tablespoons tarragon vinegar
½ teaspoon salt
Freshly ground pepper
2 teaspoons minced parsley
½ teaspoon minced tarragon, or 6 chopped anchovies and 1 puréed clove garlic

Slice mushrooms right through stem and cap to make attractive looking slices. Combine olive oil, tarragon vinegar, salt, a little freshly ground black pepper, minced parsley, and either the tarragon or the anchovies and garlic. Mix well and let stand 5 or 6 hours before serving (don't chill).

Chili Almonds

These are a nice change from the usual salted nuts.

1 pound shelled unblanched almonds
1 tablespoon chili powder
1 large clove garlic, crushed
¼ cup (⅛ lb.) butter or margarine
Coarse salt

Place almonds in a heavy pan with chili powder, garlic, and butter or margarine. Cook over medium heat, stirring constantly, until crisp and lightly browned. Remove garlic fibers, sprinkle nuts with coarse salt; cool before putting in jars.

Skewered Pineapple

Skewer chunks of fresh or frozen pineapple lengthwise on toothpick with pickled cocktail onion at the point. Or use ripe or stuffed green olives in place of onion. These may be stuck in a fresh pineapple or in a whole head of cabbage to serve.

Hot-Pepper Pecans

Hot-pepper pecans are very simple to prepare and make excellent appetizers before an elaborate dinner.

2 tablespoons butter
1 cup large pecan halves
2 teaspoons soy sauce
½ teaspoon salt
2 to 3 dashes liquid hot-pepper seasoning

Melt butter in a shallow pan. Spread pecans evenly in one layer, and bake in a slow oven (300°) for 30 minutes, or until the nuts just begin to brown. Stir several times during the baking, and be sure not to overcook. Mix soy sauce, salt, and liquid hot-pepper seasoning into toasted nuts, turning them so seasoning will be evenly distributed. Spread on a double thickness of paper towel to cool, then pack in jars with tight-fitting lids.

Cocktail Sandwiches

You can make four of these tiny sandwiches from two slices of thin bread.

1 cup minced turkey or chicken
1 cup minced smoked tongue
½ cup (¼ lb.) soft butter
Salt
Prepared mustard
9 slices white bread
9 slices whole-wheat bread

Combine turkey or chicken, tongue, butter, and salt and prepared mustard to taste. Spread on slices of white bread; top with slices of whole-wheat bread. Trim crusts and cut in 4 squares or triangles. Sandwiches may be made ahead and frozen. Makes 3 dozen appetizers.

Stuffed Carrot Curls

Consider these crisp, low-calorie appetizers for a party. If some are left over, they will be welcome additions to children's lunches or to a relish tray at lunch or dinner.

About 1 bunch carrots, peeled
2 slices bacon
1 medium-sized onion, chopped
2 hard-cooked eggs
½ cup finely shredded lettuce
1 slice fresh bread, shredded
1 tablespoon chopped parsley
½ teaspoon paprika
½ teaspoon salt
Dash of pepper
1½ teaspoons prepared mustard
2 tablespoons mayonnaise

Use a vegetable peeler to cut long, thin carrot strips, each at least 4 inches long. You should have about 50 strips. Roll around your finger and insert a toothpick to hold the curls (if they seem hard to curl, let the strips stand a few minutes in warm water). Chill in ice water for about an hour. Meanwhile, fry bacon until crisp; crumble. Sauté onion in bacon drippings until soft. In a small bowl, mash the eggs, stir in bacon and onion, then lettuce, bread, parsley, paprika, salt, pepper, mustard, and mayonnaise; mix until well blended. Shake the water from each carrot curl, and spoon stuffing (about 2 teaspoons) into center of each one. Keep in refrigerator until ready to serve. Makes about 50 appetizers.

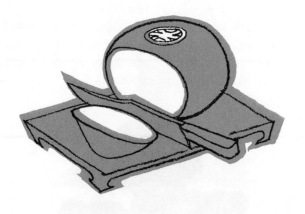

Anchovy Olives with Cherry Tomatoes

This combination of black olives and red tomatoes is as appealing to the eye as it is to the palate.

1 can (7 oz.) jumbo pitted ripe olives, drained
1 can (2 oz.) anchovy fillets, drained
2 tablespoons olive oil
1 clove garlic, puréed
⅓ cup finely minced parsley
About 1 dozen cherry tomatoes, stemmed

Stuff each olive with half an anchovy fillet. Put olives in a bowl with olive oil, garlic, and parsley. Mix well. Add cherry tomatoes, cover, and keep refrigerated until an hour before serving. Provide toothpicks to prevent oily fingers.

Ham Cubes

These delectable bits have the gay colors and stripes of a peppermint stick.

2 tablespoons prepared horseradish
2 tablespoons mayonnaise
1 teaspoon Worcestershire
½ teaspoon seasoned salt
⅛ teaspoon pepper
1 large package (8 oz.) cream cheese
6 thin slices boiled ham

Beat horseradish, mayonnaise, Worcestershire, seasoned salt, pepper, and cream cheese together until creamy and of spreading consistency. Place one ham slice on a piece of waxed paper. With a spatula, spread some of the creamed mixture over it. Place another slice of ham on top of creamed mixture and spread with more of the cheese. Repeat this process, ending with a ham slice on top, so that the ham and the spread form alternate layers in a multidecker "sandwich."

Wrap all securely in waxed paper and place in freezer or freezing compartment of refrigerator for 2 hours or more. About an hour before time to serve, remove from refrigerator and cut lengthwise and crosswise into small cubes. Pierce each cube with a colored toothpick. Place on a dish. Makes about 36 appetizers.

Green Pepper Appetizers

You start the assembly of this zesty appetizer, and your guests complete it.

4 large bell peppers
⅓ cup vinegar
¼ cup minced onion
½ teaspoon salt
¼ teaspoon pepper
½ cup olive oil or salad oil
1 clove garlic, minced
½ teaspoon dry basil
1 crumbled bay leaf
1 package (6 oz.) smoked Cheddar cheese,
    shredded
⅓ cup melted butter
60 saltine crackers

Place peppers in a hot oven (400°) until the skin puffs (about 10 to 12 minutes). Remove stems, seeds, and peel; cut in 8 slices lengthwise, then halve each slice crosswise. Combine vinegar, onion, salt, pepper, oil, garlic, basil, and bay leaf in a small bowl. Add the pepper slices, and marinate overnight in the refrigerator.

Combine cheese and the melted butter in a bowl; mix well and chill. Spread crackers generously with cheese mixture. Place marinated peppers in a nearby dish and let each guest top his own cheese-covered cracker with a piece of pepper. Makes about 60 appetizers.

Marinated Artichokes

Cook artichoke hearts until tender, immersed in boiling salted water. Drain thoroughly. While still hot, cover with a mixture of 1 part red wine vinegar and 2 parts olive oil or salad oil. For each cup of marinade, add 1 tablespoon minced onion, 1 tablespoon minced parsley, ½ teaspoon dry mustard, and 2 whole cloves garlic. Let cool. Chill overnight before using.

Seasoned cream cheese and toasted slivered almonds make little party appetizers out of fresh grapes.

Grape Appetizers

Here is a way to make tempting appetizers of fresh grapes. Use any large table grape that is available.

Stem, wash, and dry the grapes; then split each one open far enough to remove seeds. Stuff with softened cream cheese blended with salt and pepper (about ⅛ teaspoon salt and a dash of pepper for a 3-oz. package of cheese); let some of the cheese spill out the top. Toast slivered almonds until lightly browned; sprinkle with salt. Dip the stuffed grapes in the nuts; arrange on a tray and serve.

Sea Food Hors d'Oeuvre

This is a good appetizer to serve before an outdoor meal.

Fill a large bowl or tray with cracked ice. On it arrange several kinds of sea food — cooked shrimps, chunks of lobster meat, clams and oysters in their shells, raw scallops, smoked oysters, squares of smoked sturgeon, rolls of smoked salmon, and chunks of cooked finnan haddie. Have the fish, except those in shells, impaled on picks. Make the following dressing and serve in a bowl as a dunk for the sea food: Combine 1 cup mayonnaise; ¼ cup cream, whipped; ¼ cup each chili sauce, chopped green pepper, and chopped green onion. Season with salt and lemon juice.

Tuna-Anchovy Appetizer

You combine two kinds of fish for this appetizer. It is a good one to keep in mind for last-minute occasions, because it needs to marinate only 20 minutes.

1 can (7 oz.) tuna, drained
1 can (2 oz.) anchovy fillets, drained and coarsely cut
⅛ teaspoon dry mustard
⅛ teaspoon oregano
Dash cayenne
1 tablespoon pickle relish
1 teaspoon lemon juice
¼ cup French dressing

Carefully break tuna into bite-size pieces, and combine with anchovy fillets. Add mustard, oregano, cayenne, pickle relish, lemon juice, and French dressing. Marinate for 20 minutes or longer. Serve with Melba toast or crackers.

Steamed Egg Roll: Carefully lift pressed egg yolks onto egg white mixture, roll up, wrap and steam.

Steamed Egg Roll

These intricate looking appetizers are of Japanese origin. The ingredients are simple.

8 hard-cooked egg whites
¾ teaspoon salt
2¼ teaspoons sugar
4 hard-cooked egg yolks

Press egg whites through fine wire strainer; add ½ teaspoon of the salt and 2 teaspoons of the sugar. Press egg yolks through fine strainer; add remaining ¼ teaspoon salt and remaining ¼ teaspoon sugar. Pat out egg white mixture on wet cloth, shaping into a neat oblong 5 by 8 inches. Taper side away from you to a thin edge. Press yolks on a flat plate into a 3 by 7-inch oblong; move by sections, using a spatula, and arrange on top of egg whites, leaving a 1-inch margin top and bottom, ½ inch on sides. Grasping cloth with hands, quickly roll to encase yolks, pressing firmly; peel cloth as you roll. Wrap in the cloth, and tie ends securely. Steam for 8 to 10 minutes. Chill thoroughly. Unwrap and slice. Makes about 2 dozen appetizers.

Eggs Stuffed with Asparagus

Arrange these colorful stuffed eggs on a bed of parsley just before serving. They are good for calorie counters, especially if you use a low-calorie mayonnaise.

6 hard-cooked eggs
2½ tablespoons mayonnaise
2 teaspoons lemon peel
¼ teaspoon salt
⅛ teaspoon curry powder
⅛ teaspoon dry mustard
12 cooked asparagus tips
1 canned pimiento

Halve the eggs lengthwise. Remove and mash the yolks; add mayonnaise, lemon peel, salt, curry powder, and mustard, and mix until creamy. Refill the egg whites with the yolk mixture, leveling it to the flat edge of the egg. Place one asparagus tip across the center of each egg half. Cut pimiento in narrow (about ⅛ inch) strips and place two strips across each asparagus tip. Makes 12 halves.

Shrimp-stuffed Tomatoes

Tiny stuffed tomatoes can be prepared ahead and refrigerated until serving time.

1 basket cherry tomatoes
½ pound cooked, shelled shrimp
1 green onion, chopped
3 or 4 pitted black olives, chopped
1 tablespoon soy sauce

Wash and drain tomatoes; cut a thin slice off the top of each tomato and scoop out the pulp. Invert the tomatoes and set aside to drain. Chop the shrimp very fine and combine with the onion, olives, and soy sauce. Stuff this mixture into the tomato shells and refrigerate. Makes about 2½ dozen appetizers.

Crisp and refreshing, tiny tomatoes are stuffed with a chili-seasoned mixture for a colorful appetizer.

Relish-stuffed Tomatoes

Tiny tomatoes, stuffed with a spicy-crisp fresh relish, are unusual appetizers, easy to pick up in your fingers.

About 40 cherry tomatoes
1 can (4 oz.) green chilies, finely chopped
⅔ cup finely chopped celery
3 tablespoons finely chopped green onions
3 tablespoons wine vinegar
1 teaspoon sugar
Salt to taste

Cut a thin slice off the top of each tomato; scoop out inside with grapefruit knife. Make relish by combining chilies, celery, green onions, wine vinegar, sugar, and salt. Stuff tomatoes and chill. Makes about 40 appetizers.

Duchesse au Saumon

Tiny cream puffs make impressive appetizers, and they are surprisingly simple to make.

Filling:
¼ cup (⅛ lb.) soft butter
2 teaspoons minced chives
Freshly ground black pepper
½ cup finely minced smoked salmon

Cream Puffs:
¼ cup (⅛ lb.) butter
½ cup boiling water
½ cup regular all-purpose flour
2 eggs

To make filling, mix together the butter, chives, a little freshly ground black pepper, and smoked salmon.

To make the cream puffs, melt the ¼ cup butter in boiling water. Sift flour, measure, and add all at once. Stir over heat until it forms a solid mass, as it will do almost at once. Cool for 3 or 4 minutes, then stir in eggs, one at a time. The mixture will be smooth, glossy, and stiff. Arrange half-teaspoonfuls on a lightly buttered cooky sheet, 2 inches apart. Bake in a hot oven (425°) for 10 minutes; reduce heat to 350° and bake for another 8 minutes, or until dry looking and lightly golden. Cool and fill, or freeze for later use. Makes 2 dozen appetizers.

Almond Bretzels

These appetizer sticks are rich and crisp, with a toasted nut flavor. They are quick to make and easy to shape.

½ cup (¼ pound) butter or margarine
2 eggs
2 cups regular all-purpose flour
½ pound (1½ cups) almonds, finely ground
1 egg, slightly beaten
Salt (optional)

Cream butter until fluffy, add the 2 eggs, and mix well. Sift flour, measure, and add to butter and eggs along with ground nuts; stir thoroughly to blend. Roll out dough about ⅜ inch thick on a lightly floured board. Cut in strips about ⅜ inch wide and of a uniform length (not longer than 6 inches). Brush tops with beaten egg. Sprinkle with salt, if desired. Bake in a moderate oven (350°) for 15 to 20 minutes or until golden brown. Cool on racks. Makes about 5 dozen 6-inch sticks.

Roquefort-Cognac Crisps

Here's the kind of hors d'oeuvre or all-purpose snack that many a host or hostess is seeking. It is easy to serve, not too goopy, and has enough substance to be nourishing.

3 ounces Roquefort cheese
2 tablespoons butter
2 tablespoons brandy
3 red apples
Lemon juice

Mix cheese, butter, and brandy; cover and keep in refrigerator overnight or longer. Core apples but leave unpeeled. Cut into ½-inch slices and dip quickly in lemon juice to prevent darkening. If you wish apple slices that lie flat, cut each cored apple in half lengthwise, lay each half on its cut side, and slice crosswise. Spread with cheese-butter-brandy mixture and serve, with crackers on the side for those who want them. (Or spread on crackers and have apple slices on the side.)

Pickled Mushrooms

These mushroom appetizers are made by pickling small whole mushrooms with onion slices for twenty-four hours before serving.

3 pounds mushrooms
1 quart water
2 medium-sized onions, thinly sliced
½ cup distilled white vinegar
1½ teaspoons salt
½ bay leaf
¼ teaspoon whole black pepper
1 teaspoon olive oil

Cook whole or quartered mushrooms in water for 15 minutes. Drain, reserving liquid. Arrange mushrooms and onions in layers in a crock or in jars. Simmer together vinegar, mushroom liquid, salt, bay leaf, and pepper for 10 minutes, then strain over the mushrooms. Float olive oil over the top and chill for at least 24 hours before serving.

Cheese and Filbert Balls

Cheese and filbert balls are easy to make, freeze well, and are good to serve with beverages.

1 cup (¼ lb.) shredded sharp Cheddar cheese
¼ cup (⅛ lb.) butter or margarine
½ cup flour
¼ teaspoon salt
1 cup ground filberts
1 teaspoon paprika

Using your hands, mix together cheese, butter or margarine, flour, salt, ½ cup of the filberts, and paprika. When well blended, roll teaspoonfuls of the dough in little marbles, roll in the remaining ½ cup of filberts, and arrange on cooky sheets. Chill, then bake in a moderate oven (350°) for 10 minutes, or until lightly browned. Makes about 3 dozen appetizers.

Pickled small whole mushrooms, layered with onion slices, chill in jar for 24 hours to blend flavors.

Anchovy-Wrapped Radishes

Have cleaned radishes at room temperature before spreading a narrow band of softened butter around the middle of each one. Wrap a strip of anchovy around this and secure with a toothpick. Chill, then sprinkle with very finely chopped green onion to serve.

Delicious assortment of canapés are quickly made if components are in your freezer. To make easy work of a big party, keep on hand an assortment of bread bases, flavored butters, and fillings. For recipes, see pages 44 and 45.

CANAPÉS
Beautiful creations, simple to make

Curry-Coconut Canapés

You can prepare this canapé spread a day ahead. Just before serving, spread it on lengthwise-cut slices of white bread and cut into individual canapés.

1 large package (8 oz.) cream cheese
3 tablespoons finely chopped chutney
2 tablespoons chopped, preserved or candied ginger
¼ cup grated fresh coconut
½ teaspoon curry powder
Butter
3 lengthwise slices white bread, crusts trimmed, toasted if desired
Parsley for garnish

Soften cream cheese in a small bowl. Mix in until well blended the chutney, ginger, coconut, and curry powder. Spread on plain or toasted, buttered white bread; garnish with parsley. Cut into individual canapés, either triangles or fingers. Makes 30 canapés.

Hasty Hots

It takes just a few minutes to put these together.

4 green onions
½ cup grated Parmesan cheese
6 tablespoons mayonnaise
Toast rounds or sliced French rolls

Chop green onions fine. Add grated cheese and enough mayonnaise to make a spread of fairly firm consistency. Toast one side of bread rounds or roll slices. Spread mixture on untoasted side and put under broiler just until bubbly. Makes 1½ to 2 dozen canapés.

Cheese and Nut Squares

Just before serving, heat these crunchy appetizers enough to melt the cheese.

4 slices pumpernickel bread (the heavy, thin-sliced kind)
¼ cup sharp Cheddar-flavored cheese spread
1½ tablespoons chopped Brazil nuts or almonds
2 teaspoons butter or margarine

Cut bread slices in quarters. Spread each quarter evenly with cheese. Sauté nuts in butter until golden; spoon an equal amout on each section of bread and cheese. Broil until bubbling. Makes 16 canapés.

Parsley and Paprika Cheese Appetizers

These appetizers are especially complemented by dry Spanish sherry.

3 long sourdough French rolls, cut in ¼-inch slices
About 36 slices mild Cheddar cheese, about ⅛ inch thick and slightly smaller than bread slices
Grated Parmesan cheese
Dried minced parsley
Paprika

Top each slice of French bread with a piece of Cheddar cheese. Sprinkle each with a dash of Parmesan cheese; then sprinkle half of bread slices with a dash of dried minced parsley and half with a dash of paprika. Place on a baking sheet in a hot oven (400°) for 2 to 3 minutes or until cheese starts to melt. Serve hot. Makes about 36 appetizers.

Deviled Ham and Chutney Canapés

Here's a taste combination to surprise your guests —deviled ham and chutney on dark rye bread.

1 can (2¼ oz.) deviled ham
3 tablespoons finely chopped chutney
2 tablespoons mayonnaise
1 lengthwise slice dark rye bread, crusts
    trimmed, toasted

In a small bowl, combine deviled ham, chutney, and mayonnaise. Spread on toasted bread slice. Just before serving, cut into individual canapés, either triangles or fingers. Makes about 10 canapés.

Curried Crab Meat Canapés

Shredded Cheddar cheese forms the base of this curry-flavored spread. Finely chopped pimiento adds a dash of color to the rather dark canapés.

1 small can (4½ oz.) chopped ripe olives
¼ cup sliced green onions
¾ cup shredded Cheddar cheese
¼ cup mayonnaise
Pinch of salt
¼ teaspoon curry powder
8 slices white bread, crusts removed
2 tablespoons minced parsley

Mix together the olives, green onions, cheese, mayonnaise, salt, and curry powder. Toast bread lightly on both sides. Spread olive mixture on toast. Broil until bubbly. Fleck with minced parsley and cut into quarters. Makes 32 canapés.

Anchovy Puffs

Those who appreciate the saltiness of anchovy paste will appreciate these canapés.

½ cup (¼ lb.) butter or margarine
1 small package (3 oz.) cream cheese
1 cup unsifted regular all-purpose flour
3 teaspoons anchovy paste
1 teaspoon India relish
⅛ teaspoon crumbled oregano

Blend butter and cheese; mix in the flour thoroughly; chill. Roll out pastry until very thin and cut into 2-inch rounds. Combine anchovy paste, relish, and oregano, and spread lightly on top of each round. Place on a cooky sheet, and bake in a hot oven (400°) for 10 minutes. Serve piping hot. Makes 40 to 45 appetizers.

Clam and Oyster Rounds

This combination of two shellfish makes an excellent canapé.

1 small package (3 oz.) cream cheese
1 clove garlic, mashed or minced
1 tablespoon grated onion
¼ teaspoon Worcestershire
½ teaspoon salt
¼ teaspoon pepper
1 can (7 oz.) minced clams, drained
About 1 tablespoon sour cream
12 thin slices buffet rye bread or 24 small
    rye cracker rounds
2 jars (3¼ oz. each) smoked oysters
Paprika

Mash cream cheese; season with garlic, onion, Worcestershire, salt, and pepper. Add drained clams and mix well; stir in enough sour cream to make mixture spreadable but not thin. Cover each slice of bread or rye cracker with clam mixture. If using bread, cut each slice in half. Drain oysters, and if large, cut into bite-sized pieces. Put 1 or 2 pieces of oyster on top of each canapé. Sprinkle with paprika, if desired. Makes 24 canapés.

Crab Canapés

For a party, broil these crab canapés at the last minute and serve them hot.

1 jar (5 oz.) pasteurized process sharp cheese spread
1 teaspoon Worcestershire
1 tablespoon butter or margarine
½ teaspoon onion powder
Dash garlic powder
About 1 cup fresh crab meat, or 1 can (about 6½ oz.) Dungeness or King crab, drained
1 egg yolk
About 42 rounds or squares of bread, each about 2 inches across
Paprika

In a small pan, combine the cheese spread, Worcestershire, butter, onion powder, and garlic powder; stir over low heat until melted and blended. Remove from heat and add crab and egg yolk. Mix until well blended. Arrange the bread rounds or squares on a cooky sheet and put under the broiler to toast one side. Remove and spread the cheese mixture on the untoasted sides.

Just before serving, put back under the broiler (watch carefully) just until cheese mixture bubbles and lightly browns. Sprinkle lightly with paprika and serve hot. Makes about 3½ dozen canapés.

Onion-Chili Canapé

Assemble these simple, interesting canapés shortly before serving.

Spread saltines with peanut butter. Place a thin onion ring on the top of each cracker and dot the center with ½ teaspoon chili sauce.

Lengthwise bread slice, topped with well seasoned cheese mixture, cut into triangles before broiling.

Broiled Cheese Triangles

Here's a canapé to make ahead of time and freeze.

1 thin lengthwise slice bread
½ cup (packed) shredded Cheddar cheese
¼ teaspoon prepared mustard
¼ teaspoon Worcestershire
About 1 tablespoon mayonnaise
Mustard Butter (recipe on page 45)
3 slices bacon

Remove crusts from bread. Have ready a foil-covered piece of cardboard the same size as the bread slice. Blend together the cheese, prepared mustard, Worcestershire, and mayonnaise. Spread bread slice with Mustard Butter, then with the cheese mixture. Cook bacon until crisp; crumble bacon and sprinkle (to a width of about ½ inch) along both long edges of the cheese-covered bread slice; use a long straight bladed knife as a guide so you can sprinkle the bacon in an even line.

Place the bread slice on the foil-covered cardboard, set into freezer until firm, then carefully wrap and freeze. To serve, partially defrost, cut the slice lengthwise through the middle, then cut each strip into triangles. Set under broiler until lightly browned. Makes 2 dozen canapés.

Caper Cream Cheese Canapés

For best flavor, use a dark whole wheat bread for these canapés.

1 small package (3 oz.) cream cheese
1 tablespoon milk
1 tablespoon chopped capers
1 teaspoon liquid from caper bottle
⅛ teaspoon pepper
Butter
1 lengthwise slice whole wheat bread, crusts
    trimmed, toasted if desired
Chopped parsley for garnish

Soften cream cheese in small bowl. Add milk, capers, liquid from caper bottle, and pepper, creaming together well. Spread on plain or toasted, lightly buttered, dark bread; garnish with chopped parsley. Just before serving, cut into individual canapés, either triangles or fingers. Makes about 10 canapés.

Hot Raw Beef Sandwiches

If the party is informal, you can let the guests cook these hot canapés on an electric sandwich grill.

¼ cup very well drained prepared horseradish
½ cup (¼ lb.) butter
16 slices bread
1 pound raw tenderloin or sirloin steak, sliced
    very thin
Salt to taste
Soft butter

Make horseradish butter by adding prepared horseradish to the ½ cup butter. Spread on 8 slices of the bread. Top with sliced beef, sprinkle with salt, and cover with other 8 slices bread. Press firmly together, trim crusts, and brush each sandwich lightly on both sides with additional softened butter. Cook on a griddle just long enough to brown the outside without cooking the meat. Cut into quarters and serve at once. Makes about 8 sandwiches, or 32 quarters.

Mushroom Pizza

This miniature variation of Italian pizza uses split English muffins for a speedy bread base on which to pile plump mushroom caps, slivered salami, sliced stuffed olives, and cheese.

6 English muffins
⅓ cup olive or salad oil
½ tube anchovy paste
½ can (8 oz. size) tomato sauce
12 slices salami, cut in thin slivers
1 small jar stuffed green olives, sliced
1 cup small whole mushrooms, sautéed in butter
½ pound processed Cheddar cheese, sliced

Cut muffins in half with a sharp knife and brush each half with olive or salad oil. Next, spread a very thin coating of anchovy paste over the muffins; follow with a layer of tomato sauce. Arrange slivers of salami, sliced olives, and mushrooms on the muffins. Place slices of cheese over the top so that the whole muffin is covered. Bake in a moderate oven (350°) for 10 minutes, or until the cheese is melted. Cut each into quarters and serve hot. Makes 48 appetizers.

Pinwheel Canapés

You can keep these canapés in your freezer for spur-of-the-moment entertaining.

Remove crusts from a thin, lengthwise slice of bread; flatten it slightly by passing a rolling pin over it lightly. Spread with Mustard Butter (recipe on page 45), then with this filling: ½ cup shredded Cheddar cheese blended with ½ cup ground dried beef and 2 tablespoons catsup.

Or spread the bread slices with Mustard Butter, then with this filling: ½ cup liver sausage

Hot or cold these are outstanding. Keep roll in freezer and slice Pinwheel Canapés as needed.

blended with ½ teaspoon instant minced onion and 1 tablespoon mayonnaise.

Starting on the long side, roll like a jelly roll. Brush edge with soft butter, fasten roll together with toothpicks. Wrap the roll in heavy waxed paper or clear plastic wrap and pack in a box. To serve, cut ½-inch slices while the roll is still partially frozen. Serve when defrosted or broil briefly to crisp them. Makes about 20 canapés.

Hot Mushroom Bouchées

These colorful little snacks can be made ahead, stored on cooky sheets, and then broiled as needed.

2 tablespoons minced onion
1 cup sliced fresh mushrooms, or 1 can (6 or 8 oz.) whole mushrooms
¼ cup (⅛ lb.) butter or margarine
4 hard-cooked eggs, sieved
2 tablespoons minced parsley
1 teaspoon salt
⅛ teaspoon pepper
1 egg
32 small rounds of bread, toasted
½ cup shredded American cheese

Sauté onion and mushrooms in butter for about 5 minutes. Add sieved hard-cooked eggs, parsley, salt, and pepper. Beat egg slightly, stir in the hot mixture; turn back into the pan, and cook just long enough to thicken. Spread on the small toast rounds and sprinkle each one with grated cheese. Broil until cheese melts and serve hot. Makes 32 canapés.

Chutney Peanut Butter Canapés

To save time, have your bakery slice loaves of bread lengthwise for this canapé. You merely trim away crusts, then spread with soft butter and this filling.

¾ cup chunk-style peanut butter
1 small package (3 oz.) cream cheese
¼ teaspoon seasoned salt
¼ cup dry red table wine
¼ teaspoon Worcestershire
1½ cups finely chopped chutney
Butter
4 lengthwise slices pumpernickel bread, crusts trimmed, toasted

Blend well the peanut butter, cream cheese, seasoned salt, wine, and Worcestershire. Add chutney and mix well. Spread on buttered toasted pumpernickel bread. Just before serving, cut bread into individual canapés, either triangles or fingers. Makes about 40 canapés.

Bread bases, spreads, and garnishes from the freezer: left to right, green butter spread with whole shrimp; ham filling with walnut; anchovy with crab claw.

CANAPÉS FROM THE FREEZER

To make easy work of a big party (or to be prepared for spur-of-the-moment entertaining), fill your freezer gradually with a variety of butters, fillings, and bread bases that can be assembled quickly in many different combinations to give you a wide selection of canapés. Add an assortment of toppings and garnishes, packed in small containers and tucked into corners of the freezer.

Foundations for Appetizers

The bread bases should be thawed briefly before spreading. Lightly toast the puffs, then split and fill.

Bread bases: Cut unsliced bread—white, or several kinds, including rye and whole wheat—into lengthwise slices about ⅓-inch thick; this is easier if you partially freeze it first. Using cooky cutters or a sharp knife, cut out rounds, fingers, squares, triangles, or other fancy shapes.

To make double-decker cases, use a small round cutter or large thimble to cut holes in the centers of some of the rounds, and place the rims on top of whole rounds.

To freeze, stack with waxed paper in plastic containers, or use foil-lined boxes and overwrap with more foil. Label.

Cocktail puffs: Bring 1 cup water to a boil. Add ¼ pound (½ cup) butter. When melted, stir in 1 cup sifted flour. Continue to stir briskly over moderate heat until the dough gathers into a ball. While dough cools, beat 4 eggs until very thick; add to cooled dough and blend thoroughly. Drop from a teaspoon onto greased cooky sheet. Bake in a hot oven (400°) for about 15 minutes; cool on a rack. Makes about 60 puffs.

When thoroughly cool, freeze in plastic containers, or seal in plastic bags. (Note: Puffs made by this different method stay especially crisp after freezing.)

Flavored Butters

Bread cut-outs can be spread with plain butter, of course, when you are going to add a filling, but these flavored butters will add extra character. Use them, too, with plain toppings—sliced meats, cheeses, and sea foods. Wrap butters securely in foil or clear plastic wrap. You can open the packages and slice off what you need while they are still frozen.

Mustard Butter: Beat ¼ pound firm butter (sweet or salted) until the consistency of whipped cream. Beat in 2 to 3 tablespoons prepared mustard. Wrap and freeze. Very good with ham, tongue, or liver pâté.

Anchovy or Sardine Butter: Beat ¼ pound sweet butter to the consistency of whipped cream. Add 2 tablespoons light cream and 1 tablespoon either anchovy paste or sardine paste. (If you don't have paste, wash oil from fillets, remove bones, and mash to a paste.) Wrap and freeze. Good with sea food such as crab, lobster, or tuna.

Almond Butter: Whip ¼ pound butter until creamy. Add 2 tablespoons light cream and ½ cup finely ground almonds; blend well. Wrap and freeze. A good base for any fish, shellfish, or chicken.

Green Butter: Beat ¼ pound salted butter until creamy. Blend in 2 tablespoons light cream, ¼ teaspoon salt, and ¼ cup minced parsley. Add a few drops of green food coloring, if desired, but use a light hand, for coloring tends to darken as it stands. Colorful base for tuna, shrimp, or crab or lobster meat.

Spreads and Fillings

Pack these in rigid freezer containers or wrap in heavy foil or clear plastic wrap.

Blue Cheese Filling: Using your electric mixer, blend together 1 large package (8 oz.) cream cheese, ¼ pound blue or Roquefort cheese, and 1 tablespoon light cream. Package and freeze.

Tuna Filling: Drain 1 can (6 or 7 oz.) tuna and break into a bowl. Blend in 1 package (3 oz.) cream cheese (or cream cheese with chives), 2 tablespoons

chopped pimiento, ½ teaspoon smoke-seasoned salt, dash of pepper. Package and freeze.

Meat Filling: To 2½ cups ground leftover roast beef, pork, or veal, add 2 tablespoons grated onion, 1 teaspoon chili powder, 1 tablespoon minced green pepper, ½ cup tomato purée, 1 tablespoon mayonnaise, ¼ teaspoon prepared mustard, and salt to taste. Blend thoroughly. Package and freeze.

Ham Filling: To 1 cup of ground ham, add 2 teaspoons brown sugar, ¼ teaspoon dry mustard, 1 tablespoon each minced green onion, parsley, and pimiento, ¼ cup minced sweet pickle, and 2 tablespoons mayonnaise. Blend well. Package and freeze.

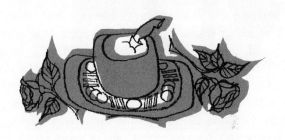

Garnishes That Freeze Well

Here are a few examples of garnishes that can be frozen and used to give variety to canapés : Small slices of lobster tail; colorful crab claw segments; whole shrimp, cooked in flavorful stock; smoke-cooked turkey breast; cooked ham or tongue; sieved egg yolk; chopped ripe or green olives; chopped parsley or chives; and chopped nuts.

Quick-Combination Appetizers

These appetizers can be combined quickly from the basic foundations, butters, and fillings given above. Use your imagination to create others.

Puffs, each stuffed with cheese filling and a small whole shrimp.

Puffs, each stuffed with tuna filling and a slice of stuffed olive.

Finger-shaped bread cut-outs, almond butter spread, thin-sliced chicken or turkey breast, or crab claw.

Rosette bread cut-outs, anchovy butter spread, tuna filling, garnish of pimiento strip on top.

Triangle bread cut-outs, green butter spread, small shrimp, parsley garnish.

Bread case, mustard butter spread, ham filling in cavity.

Ham Puffs

These hot canapés are quick to make. They can be made ahead and then frozen.

1 large package (8 oz.) cream cheese, softened
1 egg yolk
1 teaspoon baking powder
Dash of salt
10 to 12 thin slices white sandwich bread
Mayonnaise
1 large can (4½ oz.) deviled ham
Paprika

Combine cream cheese with egg yolk, baking powder, and salt; mix until blended and smooth. Cut about 4 small rounds from each slice of the bread, using a biscuit cutter. Spread each round lightly with mayonnaise. Spread each with a thin layer of deviled ham. Spoon the cheese mixture on the ham, and sprinkle with paprika. This much can be done ahead and the appetizers frozen, if you wish. To serve, put into a moderately hot oven (375°) for 12 to 15 minutes, or until puffed and browned. Serve immediately. Makes about 45 appetizers.

Olympia Oyster Canapé

You serve one tiny Olympia oyster and some of the tangy butter sauce on each of these round toast canapés.

⅓ cup butter or margarine
2 teaspoons prepared mustard
2 teaspoons Worcestershire
1 tablespoon finely chopped parsley
⅛ teaspoon salt
1 cup Olympia oysters or drained tiny smoked oysters
50 rounds of bread, each 1 inch in diameter

Melt butter or margarine over low heat; add prepared mustard, Worcestershire, parsley, and salt. You can prepare this much ahead.

Just before serving, add oysters to the sauce and place over low heat about one minute, or just until oysters are hot. Meanwhile, cut rounds of bread and toast under broiler on both sides. Place one oyster on each toast round and spoon some of the butter sauce over each. You may also serve these oysters in tiny patty shells instead of on toast rounds. Makes about 50 canapés.

Curried Crab Meat Canapés

Curry and Parmesan cheese give sharp flavor to these broiled crab canapés.

½ teaspoon minced onion
2 tablespoons butter or margarine
1½ teaspoons flour
½ teaspoon curry powder
⅛ teaspoon salt
¼ cup light cream
½ cup well-flaked crab meat
4 thin slices toasted bread, crusts removed
3 tablespoons grated Parmesan cheese

Sauté onion in butter until lightly browned. Combine flour, curry powder, and salt, and stir into onion; cook until bubbly. Slowly pour in cream, stirring constantly. Mix in crab meat. Cut toast slices into quarters. Spread crab mixture on toast squares and sprinkle with cheese. Place on a cooky sheet and broil until cheese melts. Serve hot. Makes 16 canapés.

Green Pepper-Cheese Broil

Flecks of green pepper and crumbled bacon flavor these cheese canapés.

1 slice bacon, diced
¼ cup (⅛ lb.) butter or margarine
1 package (3 oz.) pimiento cream cheese
3 tablespoons finely chopped green pepper
1 clove garlic, mashed or minced
1 egg slightly beaten
8 thin slices bread, crusts trimmed

Fry bacon until crisp. Cream butter or margarine with cream cheese. Stir in bacon and drippings, green pepper, and garlic. Stir in slightly beaten egg, blending thoroughly. Cut bread slices into quarters or narrow strips. Toast one side of bread quarters or strips under broiler; remove from oven. Turn bread over and spread cheese mixture on untoasted side. Return to oven and broil until cheese bubbles and browns slightly. Serve hot. Makes about 32 canapés.

Sardine Canapés

These handsome finger-size sandwiches are hearty with robust flavor. Sardines are arranged individually on toast strips spread with a mild onion cream, then garnished with red tomato or pimiento.

Soft butter
4 slices white bread, toasted, crusts removed
1 tablespoon minced onion
1 tablespoon minced chives
3 tablespoons sour cream
1 can (3 ¾ oz.) Norwegian or brisling sardines
    packed in oil, drained
Very thin tomato wedges or pimiento strips

Butter each slice of toast on one side. Cut each slice in three strips. Blend together onion, chives, and sour cream and spread on toast strips. Top each with a drained sardine; garnish with thin tomato wedges or pimiento strips. Makes 12 canapés.

Mushroom slices, coated in thick brown cream and served on toast rounds, make a hit with party guests.

Hot Mushroom Canapés

These canapés are rich, delicious, and quite easy to make.

5 large mushrooms, about 2½ inches in diameter
Salt
1 cup heavy cream
20 to 25 small rounds of bread, toasted

Slice mushrooms from top to bottom, including stems. Save the slices without stems for another purpose, and put remaining slices in a heavy saucepan. Sprinkle lightly with salt and barely cover with cream. Put over high heat; as soon as the cream boils up, turn the heat to a low simmer and cook, stirring occasionally, until the cream is very thick and browned.

Transfer to a chafing dish and keep hot. For each canapé, put a slice of mushroom, well covered with brown cream, on a round of toast just before serving. Makes 20 to 25 appetizers.

Shells of avocado, lobster, Gouda, green pepper make attractive serving containers for dips and spreads. Front to back: Camembert, guacamole, caraway role, lobster, chili-egg, and Gouda cheese. Chili-egg recipe on page 50, all others pages 52, 53.

SPREADS AND DIPS
Artfully seasoned, attractive to serve

Smoked Oyster and Cheese Spread

Crisp toast rounds are a good base for this smoked oyster cheese. Let guests spread their own so that the appetizers will be crisp.

1 small package (3 oz.) cream cheese
1 small jar (4 oz.) smoked oysters, chopped
1 tablespoon mayonnaise
1 tablespoon sherry or milk
1 teaspoon onion juice
½ teaspoon paprika
Finely minced chives

Mix the cheese, oysters, mayonnaise, sherry, onion juice, and paprika. Pile into a serving dish. Chill. Serve sprinkled with chopped chives. Makes 1 cup.

Pecan-coated Cheese Ball

This nut-covered cheese ball is about the size of a grapefruit. It looks handsome on an hors d'oeuvre tray with your favorite crackers.

1 large package (8 oz.) cream cheese
1 small jar (5 oz.) processed sharp cheese spread
2 jars (5 oz. each) processed Roquefort cheese spread
1 small onion, minced
1 clove garlic, minced or mashed
½ cup chopped pecans or walnuts

Let cheeses warm to room temperature, then beat together until light and fluffy and blended. Beat in the onion and garlic. Chill. Roll into a ball then roll in chopped nuts until well coated. Keep in refrigerator until needed.

Crab-Water Chestnut Appetizer

Serve this appetizer with crisp crackers and a beverage.

1 pound fresh crab meat, chopped
½ cup minced water chestnuts
2 tablespoons soy sauce
½ cup mayonnaise
2 tablespoons minced green onions

Combine crab meat with water chestnuts, soy sauce, mayonnaise, and onions. Makes about 3 cups.

Chicken Liver-Mushroom Pâté

Serve this creamy pâté with a selection of crisp crackers.

¼ cup (⅛ lb.) butter
½ pound fresh mushrooms
1 pound chicken livers
1 teaspoon garlic salt
1 teaspoon paprika
⅓ cup finely chopped green onion
⅓ cup white table wine
$\frac{1}{16}$ teaspoon dill weed
3 drops liquid hot-pepper seasoning
½ cup (¼ lb.) butter
Salt to taste

Simmer for 5 minutes in the ¼ cup butter the mushrooms, chicken livers, garlic salt, paprika, and onion. Add wine, dill weed, and liquid hot-pepper seasoning; cover and cook slowly for 5 to 10 minutes longer. Cool, and sieve or whirl smooth in a blender. Blend in the ½ cup butter and salt. Turn into serving dish and chill overnight. Makes about 3 cups.

Herb Cheese

This green-flecked cheese spread is flavored with an excellent blend of herbs.

2 pounds sharp Cheddar cheese, shredded
2 tablespoons minced parsley
2 tablespoons minced chives
2 tablespoons thyme
2 tablespoons sage
2 tablespoons savory
½ cup whipping cream
1 cup sherry

Blend well by hand, or with an electric mixer, the cheese, parsley, chives, thyme, sage, savory, cream, and sherry. Refrigerate 3 days; force through strainer or whirl in blender. Makes about 5 cups.

Chili-Egg Spread

A large green pepper, with top cut off and seeds removed, might be used to serve this spread. Cut a thin slice off the bottom of the pepper so it will stand upright.

8 hard-cooked eggs, chopped
½ cup mayonnaise
2 teaspoons lemon juice
1 tablespoon finely chopped onion
1 teaspoon chili powder
1 teaspoon Worcestershire
½ teaspoon prepared mustard
Salt to taste

Blend all the ingredients. Refrigerate for several hours to blend flavors. Garnish with pimiento, if you wish. Makes about 2 cups.

Smoked Salmon Pâté

You can either spread this pâté on round salted crackers or serve it molded, providing crackers and a spreader.

2 medium-sized potatoes, peeled, boiled, cubed
1 can (6½ oz.) smoked salmon
3 anchovy fillets
⅓ cup melted butter
1 tablespoon poppy seed
1 tablespoon celery seed
1 teaspoon freshly ground black pepper
½ teaspoon monosodium glutamate
About ½ cup mayonnaise
Chopped chives

Combine the cubed potatoes (about 1½ cups), salmon and anchovy fillets; put through a food chopper using the finest blade, or whirl in an electric blender. Spoon mixture into a bowl and stir in the butter, poppy seed, celery seed, pepper, and monosodium glutamate.

If you plan to spread the pâté on crackers, chill it until you are ready to use. If you want to serve it as a frosted mold, pack it in a buttered 1-pint mold or loaf pan and chill in refrigerator. Just before serving, run a knife around the edge of the mold or pan to unmold; spread it with mayonnaise and sprinkle sides and top with chopped chives. Makes about 2 cups.

Liverwurst Pâté

Serve this appetizer to spread on Melba toast.

1 package (8 oz.) liver-flavored sausage
6 slices bacon, cooked and crumbled
2 tablespoons finely chopped green onion, including some of the tops
1 tablespoon sherry
2 tablespoons soft butter or margarine

Mash sausage with a fork. Stir in bacon, onion, sherry, and soft butter or margarine. Pack into a heavy ceramic container and chill well. Makes about 1 cup.

Black Bean Cracker Spread

This quickly prepared spread is most convenient to blend in an attractive frying pan or saucepan that can be brought directly to the living room and kept warm on an electric trivet or tray.

1 can (10½ oz.) black bean soup
1 can (8 oz.) tomato sauce
½ to 1 cup shredded, sharp Cheddar cheese
¼ teaspoon chili powder

Combine black bean soup, tomato sauce, ½ cup of the cheese, and the chili powder. Cook over medium heat until the cheese has melted. Add more shredded cheese until the spread is as thick as you desire. Serve warm as a spread for crackers or as a dip for chips or crackers. Makes about 2½ cups.

Shrimp Spread

Serve this appetizer on thinly sliced rye bread, pumpernickel, or crisp rye crackers.

1 pound shelled cooked shrimp
2 stalks celery, including the tops
2 sprigs parsley
¼ green pepper
⅛ teaspoon liquid hot-pepper seasoning, or to taste
¼ teaspoon garlic salt
Pepper to taste
½ teaspoon paprika
About 5 tablespoons mayonnaise

Use a blender, or a food chopper with a medium blade, to cut shrimp, celery, parsley, and green pepper. Add all remaining ingredients, with the mayonnaise last, so you can add more of it if needed to give mixture a good spreading consistency. Makes about 2 cups.

Red Cheese Ball

To make this colorful appetizer, you press the well-seasoned cheese mixture into the shape of a ball, then roll it in coarsely snipped dried beef. Surround it on a plate with crisp crackers or small rye bread slices, and provide spreaders for your guests to help themselves.

½ pound natural Cheddar cheese, finely shredded
1 package (3 oz.) cream cheese, softened
3 tablespoons sherry
¼ cup pitted ripe olives, coarsely chopped
½ teaspoon Worcestershire
Dash each of onion salt, garlic salt, and celery salt
½ cup dried beef, coarsely snipped

Using your electric mixer, beat together the Cheddar and cream cheese. Add the sherry, olives, Worcestershire, and the seasoning salts; continue beating until well blended. Turn out on foil or waxed paper and use your hands to round it into a ball. Wrap it in the foil or waxed paper and refrigerate (it is a good idea to keep the cheese ball in your refrigerator for several days so the flavors will blend). About 30 minutes before you plan to serve the cheese, unwrap and reshape it, if needed. Then roll it in the dried beef until completely coated. Makes a ball about 3 inches in diameter.

Potted Cheese

Spread this appetizer on coarse-textured pumpernickel bread and offer green onions and salted almonds. It is especially delicious served with sherry.

2 cups shredded sharp Cheddar cheese
1 cup crumbled Gorgonzola or blue cheese
½ cup (¼ lb.) soft butter
⅓ cup dry sherry

Beat together Cheddar cheese, Gorgonzola or blue cheese, butter, and sherry. Pack in a small container. Cover and chill at least 24 hours. Makes about 2 cups.

Camembert Spread or Dip

You might pile this dip into a lettuce shell and garnish it with thinly sliced radishes. It is especially good with Melba rye toast or buffet-sized slices of rye bread.

1 large package (8 oz.) cream cheese, softened
1 package (4 oz.) soft Camembert cheese
2 cups small curd cottage cheese
⅓ cup grated Parmesan cheese
About 1 teaspoon seasoned salt
Toasted sesame seeds or dill seeds (optional)

Beat together the cream cheese and the Camembert (including the skin) until smooth. Combine with cottage cheese, Parmesan cheese, and seasoned salt to taste. Sprinkle sesame or dill seed on top, if you wish. Makes about 3½ cups.

Gouda Cheese Spread

This appetizer is served in a Gouda cheese shell. For a more festive looking shell, cut the edge in a zigzag or scalloped pattern.

1 whole Gouda or Edam cheese
1 cup sour cream
⅓ cup white table wine or chicken broth
2 teaspoons grated onion
¼ cup finely chopped green pepper
¼ cup finely chopped pimiento
Seasoned salt to taste

Cut a ½ to 1-inch-thick slice from top of cheese. Using a spoon or knife with a curved blade, scoop out cheese, leaving a firm shell. Shred cheese very fine and measure. You should have 1 quart. Combine cheese with sour cream, wine, and grated onion. Beat until fluffy and well blended. Stir in green pepper, pimiento, and seasoned salt. Pile lightly back into the cheese shell. Makes about 3½ cups.

Holiday Guacamole

You can use the avocado shells to serve this dip.

1 can (7 oz.) minced clams
2 medium-sized avocados
1 small clove garlic, minced or mashed
1 small onion, finely chopped
1 canned green chili (optional)
1 tablespoon lime juice
1 teaspoon seasoned salt
2 tablespoons clam liquor
1 medium-sized tomato, peeled and finely
    chopped

Drain clams, saving liquor. Cut avocados in half lengthwise; then remove the seeds and scoop out the pulp, saving shells. Combine avocado pulp, garlic, onion, and the stemmed and chopped green chili (if used). Add lime juice, salt, and the 2 tablespoons clam liquor; whirl in an electric blender until smooth, or mash ingredients thoroughly together. Add tomato and the drained clams; mix well. Makes 1½ to 2 cups.

Crab and Olive Spread

Chopped ripe olives extend the crab in this spread. Flake the crab meat well so the mixture has a fluffy consistency.

1 cup flaked crab meat (well packed in cup)
1 can (4½ oz.) chopped ripe olives
2 hard-cooked eggs, coarsely chopped
¼ cup mayonnaise
1 tablespoon Worcestershire
2 tablespoons lemon juice
2 teaspoons prepared horseradish
2 teaspoons catsup
1 teaspoon minced chives

Place the crab meat, chopped olives, chopped eggs, mayonnaise, Worcestershire, lemon juice, horseradish, and catsup into a bowl; mix until well blended. Spoon spread into a serving bowl and sprinkle with minced chives. Provide a butter knife and serve with crisp whole wheat or rye crackers or corn chips. Makes 1½ cups.

Caraway Roll

This roll is right for spreading. You can also use it as a dip by thinning the mixture with additional cream or beer and then beating it until fluffy.

1 large package (8 oz.) cream cheese, softened
⅓ cup cream or beer
¾ pound jack cheese, finely shredded
1 tablespoon caraway seed
1 teaspoon seasoned salt
⅓ cup shredded Parmesan cheese

Blend into cream cheese the cream or beer, and beat until fluffy. Add jack cheese, caraway seeds, and seasoned salt, adding more salt to taste if desired. Mix well and spoon onto foil or wax paper that has been sprinkled with the Parmesan cheese. Shape into a log, coating the outside with shredded cheese. (If the mixture is too soft to handle, chill a short time until you can shape it.) Chill until firm, 2 hours or more. Makes about 3 cups.

Lobster Spread or Dip

A colorful way to serve this dip is to pile it into an empty lobster shell or tail.

1 large package (8 oz.) cream cheese, softened
2 tablespoons crumbled Roquefort or blue cheese
½ cup sour cream
½ clove garlic, mashed, or a dash of garlic powder
2 teaspoons instant minced onion or 2 tablespoons finely chopped green onion
1 tablespoon lemon juice
1 tablespoon water
1 can (6½ oz.) lobster or 1 cup fresh or frozen lobster meat
Chopped parsley

Into the cream cheese, beat the Roquefort cheese, sour cream, garlic, onion, lemon juice, and water. Stir in lobster meat (and its liquor, if canned meat is used), breaking up the larger pieces. If you use fresh lobster, you may wish to thin the mixture slightly with cream. Pile into a serving dish and sprinkle with chopped parsley. Makes about 2 cups.

Samsoe cheese is blended with butter, mustard, and Kummel to make this attractive appetizer cheese ball.

Samsoe Cheese Ball

This cheese ball is attractively coated with toasted sesame seed. The recipe yields a 4½-inch ball, but if you divide the recipe in half, the ball will still be a respectable 3¼ inches in diameter.

¼ cup sesame seed
1 pound Samsoe or Gruyère cheese, finely shredded
1 cup (½ lb.) soft butter
1 teaspoon prepared Dijon-style mustard
2 tablespoons Kummel, Aquavit, or gin
Watercress or parsley
Radish roses

Toast sesame seed by spreading them in a shallow baking pan or cooky sheet. Place in a moderate oven (350°) for about 5 minutes or until golden.

Blend cheese with butter, mustard, and Kummel to make a smooth mixture. Shape with palms of hands into a ball. Coat with toasted sesame seed. Wrap in clear plastic film and chill until firm, several hours or overnight. Garnish with a wreath of watercress or parsley and radishes. Makes a 4½-inch ball.

Curry-Sour Cream Dip for Tiny Tomatoes

Serve this dip in a "bowl" made of a hollowed-out large tomato. Spear red or yellow pear tomatoes or cherry tomatoes on toothpicks and stick them, pincushion-style, into another large tomato.

1 cup sour cream
1 teaspoon curry powder
Dash of salt
¼ teaspoon powdered ginger
1 teaspoon honey
1 tablespoon lemon juice
2 large firm ace or beefsteak tomatoes
Pear tomatoes, about half red and half yellow,
    or red cherry tomatoes

In a small bowl, combine sour cream with curry powder, salt, ginger, honey, and lemon juice. Let stand for about 30 minutes to allow flavors to mellow and combine.

Herb Dip

Serve this dip with an assortment of raw vegetables for dunking—cherry tomatoes, cucumber sticks, sliced raw turnips, cauliflowerets, green pepper strips.

2 cups (1 pt.) prepared chive sour cream
    dressing
1 teaspoon caraway seed
2 teaspoons instant minced onion
Salt and pepper to taste

Blend prepared chive sour cream dressing with caraway seed and instant minced onion. Add salt and pepper to taste. Chill several hours before serving. Makes 2 cups dip.

To make tomato bowl, slice about ¼ of the way down from top of one of the large tomatoes. With a spoon, hollow out the inside and invert onto a dish or paper towel to drain. Fill with the sour cream dip, and chill until serving time. Makes 1 cup dip.

When ready to serve, place the other large tomato, stem-end down, on serving tray. Spear the small pear or cherry tomatoes with toothpicks, and stick them into it.

Red and yellow pear tomatoes, served with curry-flavored dip in bowl made from hollowed tomato.

Beef Tartare Loaf

To be authentic, the raw beef should be scraped for this spread; if you don't have that kind of patience, trim off the fat and grind the beef, using the fine blade of the food chopper.

5 pounds sirloin or other tender beef, trimmed and
    ground
4 or 5 egg yolks, slightly beaten
3 medium-sized onions, finely minced
5 teaspoons salt
1 teaspoon freshly ground pepper
½ cup minced parsley
Chives
Capers

Mix beef with egg yolks, onions, salt, pepper, and parsley. When thoroughly blended, form in a loaf or long roll and sprinkle with minced chives. Stud with whole capers. Serves about 50 when accompanied by other foods.

Borsos Tojas

Here is a simple, appealing appetizer from Hungary. Garnish it with radish roses and green onions with their leaves fringed. Serve it with thin-sliced pumpernickel bread.

8 hard-cooked eggs, chopped
¼ cup (⅛ lb.) soft butter
2 teaspoons prepared mustard
2 teaspoons paprika
Salt and pepper to taste
Paprika for garnish

Mix eggs with butter, prepared mustard, paprika, and salt and pepper to taste. Press into a small mold and chill. Flavors improve if the mold is chilled overnight. Unmold, sprinkle with paprika. Makes about 2 cups.

Chopped Chicken Liver Pâté

This creamy pâté is especially delicious on rye bread. Most meat markets sell chicken fat, and it gives this pâté a better flavor; however, if you can't get it, substitute butter.

8 large onions, minced
1 cup chicken fat or butter
3 pounds chicken livers
8 hard-cooked eggs, chopped
Salt and pepper

Cook onions in the chicken fat until brown. Add chicken livers; cook until they have lost most of their pinkness. (If some of the onions become black, that's to the good; they give a desired flavor.) Cool slightly and chop rather fine. Add chopped eggs and salt and pepper to taste. If the mixture is not moist enough, add more chicken fat or butter. Makes enough to serve 50.

Stuffed Gouda Cheese

This spread is made by hollowing out a baby Gouda cheese and whipping its contents with butter and seasonings. It is especially complemented by thin slices of firm Westphalian pumpernickel bread.

14-ounce baby Gouda cheese
½ cup beer
1 teaspoon prepared Dijon-style mustard
⅛ teaspoon nutmeg
¼ cup soft butter, cut in chunks
½ teaspoon caraway seed

Cut out a circle from center of top of the cheese. Carefully scoop out the cheese inside, leaving the shell intact. Use a curved small knife, such as a grapefruit knife, to remove the cheese when you begin the process; finish the job carefully with a spoon to avoid puncturing the casing.

Place ¼ cup of the beer in a blender. Cut the larger pieces of cheese into cubes; add all the cheese to blender with mustard, nutmeg, and butter. Blend until smooth, adding remaining beer gradually with motor running; stir down with spatula occasionally. Fold in caraway seed. Spoon cheese mixture into the shell; refill later with the remainder. This cheese mixture can be made as much as 24 hours before serving and refrigerated. The flavor, however, does not improve if held longer. Makes 1½ cups filling.

Shrimp Dip

Surround this dip with crisp potato and corn chips.

½ pound processed Cheddar cheese
1 can (5 oz.) shrimp
1 small onion
1 cup mayonnaise
1 teaspoon Worcestershire
Dash of garlic salt

Run through a food chopper the cheese, shrimp, and onion. Mix with mayonnaise, Worcestershire, and dash of garlic salt. Store in cool place. Makes about 4 cups dip.

Chafing Dish Clam Dip

Have all the ingredients on hand, and make this hot clam dip in a chafing dish while guests look on and enjoy the fragrant aromas.

4 slices bacon, chopped
1 small clove garlic, minced or mashed
1 can (7 oz.) minced clams, undrained
2 teaspoons cornstarch
½ teaspoon basil, crumbled
¼ cup tomato purée
¼ teaspoon salt
⅛ teaspoon pepper
2 teaspoons minced parsley
2 tablespoons grated or shredded Parmesan
    cheese
Potato chips or hard French rolls

In a chafing dish (or an electric frying pan), cook bacon and garlic over moderate heat until bacon is crisp and lightly browned. Drain off all but about 2 tablespoons bacon drippings. Add clams, blended with cornstarch, basil, tomato purée, salt, pepper, and parsley. Cook, stirring, until thickened and simmering. Blend in cheese; keep warm in a hot water bath or over very low heat. (If mixture thickens too much, stir in a little milk.) Serve as a dip for potato chips or thin slices of hard French rolls. Makes about 1¼ cups dip.

Raw Mushroom Dip

The distinctive essence of fresh mushrooms is shown off to excellent advantage in this simple creamy mixture. Serve it as a dip or spread for canapés.

2 packages (3 oz. each) cream cheese
1 tablespoon minced onion
1 cup finely chopped raw mushrooms
½ teaspoon salt
Dash monosodium glutamate (optional)
Minced parsley
Crisp crackers

Whip cream cheese and onion until light and fluffy. Stir in mushrooms, salt, and monosodium glutamate. Sprinkle with parsley. Serve as a dip for crisp crackers, or use as a spread for tiny open-faced wheat bread sandwiches, garnished with parsley. Makes about 2 cups dip.

Curried Egg Dip for Shrimp

This dip has just the right amount of seasoning to complement shrimp or other sea food.

1 cup mayonnaise
1 hard-cooked egg, very finely chopped
1 teaspoon grated fresh ginger root or ½
    teaspoon powdered ginger
1 clove garlic
½ teaspoon salt
2 tablespoons finely chopped green onion
    and tops
1 teaspoon curry powder
1 teaspoon lemon juice
Cooked prawns, lobster meat, or crab legs

Mix together thoroughly the mayonnaise, chopped egg, and ginger. Peel garlic and crush thoroughly with the salt (or mash garlic and mix with salt, or add it separately). Add garlic and salt, onion, curry powder, and lemon juice, and blend well. (If you like a very smooth dip, mix this in your blender.) Spoon into a dish, surround with prawns, and let each guest "dunk" his own sea food. This spread is also good on crisp crackers. Makes about 1½ cups dip.

Walnut Ham Spread

Walnuts impart a subtle flavor to this classic ham spread.

⅓ cup mayonnaise
1 slice onion
1 cup cubed cooked ham
¼ cup broken walnuts
½ teaspoon dry mustard
Chopped walnuts for garnish

Place ingredients in blender in the order given. Blend until mixture is smooth, stirring it down occasionally with a rubber spatula. Sprinkle with additional chopped walnuts to serve. Makes about 1 cup.

Trio of spreads: Watercress sprigs garnish Watercress and Dried Beef Spread; chopped walnuts encircle Walnut Ham Spread; dill weed tops Herring Spread.

Watercress and Dried Beef Spread

To retain the bright colors of the watercress and dried beef in this melange, it's best to chop them with a French knife or kitchen scissors rather than a blender. You can use an electric mixer, however, to beat the cream cheese base mixture.

1 jar (2½ oz.) dried beef, chopped
Boiling water
2 tablespoons mayonnaise
1 tablespoon prepared horseradish
4 ounces (half of 8-oz. package) soft cream cheese
½ cup finely chopped watercress

Place dried beef in a wire strainer and pour boiling water through it; drain well. Beat mayonnaise, horseradish, and cream cheese until fluffy. Fold in dried beef and watercress. Makes about 1 cup.

Herring Spread

Those who are fond of marinated herring will particularly enjoy this spread, made easily in a blender. Drain the herring well and remove the bay leaf if there is one, but include the tangy onions.

2 tablespoons heavy cream
Dash of liquid hot-pepper seasoning
2 tablespoons chopped chives or sliced green onion
¼ teaspoon dill weed
⅛ teaspoon paprika
4 ounces (half of 8-oz. package) soft cream cheese, cubed
6-ounce jar marinated herring in wine sauce (with onions), well drained
Dill weed

Place all ingredients in blender and whirl until mixture is smooth, stirring down occasionally with a rubber spatula. Sprinkle with additional dill weed to serve. Makes about 1 cup.

Tomato Crab Spread

A blender is used for this smooth and tangy flavored sea food combination. Stir in the crab meat at the last to preserve its identity.

1 tablespoon tomato paste
1 tablespoon water
2 teaspoons lemon juice
4 ounces (half of 8-oz. package) soft cream
   cheese, cubed
⅛ teaspoon garlic powder
Dash of pepper
½ teaspoon salt
¼ teaspoon liquid hot-pepper seasoning
1 cup (about 4 oz.) drained, flaked, cooked
   crab meat
Chopped parsley

Place all ingredients except crab and parsley in blender in the order given. Blend until the mixture is smooth, stirring it down occasionally with a rubber spatula. Fold in crab meat, and sprinkle with a border of chopped parsley to serve. Makes about 1 cup.

Rumaki Spread

The flavors of the popular Japanese hot appetizer, *rumaki*, are retained in this chicken liver spread. Although chilling improves the flavor of the mixture, it needs to soften at room temperature for at least an hour in order to spread easily on crisp, thin crackers.

1 tablespoon soy sauce
½ pound chicken livers, cooked and drained
½ cup (¼ lb.) soft butter, cubed
½ teaspoon onion salt
½ teaspoon dry mustard
¼ teaspoon nutmeg
Dash cayenne
1 can (5 oz.) water chestnuts, well drained
   and finely chopped
6 slices crisp cooked bacon, crumbled
Thinly sliced green onions

Place soy sauce, livers, butter, onion, salt, mustard, nutmeg, and cayenne in blender. Blend until mixture is smooth, stirring it down occasionally with a rubber spatula. Stir in water chestnuts and bacon. Garnish with onions. Makes about 1½ cups.

Bagna Cauda

This robust appetizer dip is particularly well suited to outdoor meals. It can be made in a saucepan over the charcoal, or in a small chafing dish.

1 cup (½ lb.) butter
½ cup olive oil
4 to 8 puréed cloves garlic
2 cans (2 oz. each) anchovy fillets, chopped in
   small pieces
Celery sticks, chilled
Carrot sticks, chilled
Cauliflower pieces (cauliflowerets), chilled
Green pepper strips, chilled
Raw green beans, chilled (optional)

Combine butter, olive oil, garlic, and anchovy fillets. Heat gently for 10 minutes, but do not allow to boil or brown.

Serve the dip, piping hot, with an ice cold assortment of the celery and carrot sticks, cauliflowerets, strips of green pepper, and if you wish, raw green beans. Makes 1½ cups dip.

Fondue Neufchâteloise

Since this classic dish is best if made in fairly small batches, this recipe serves about 20 people when other food is served. If you wish to serve a larger group, have on hand additional shredded cheese and extra ingredients in proportional amounts.

1 clove garlic, peeled
5 cups light white table wine (such as Riesling
    or Traminer)
2½ pounds Switzerland Swiss cheese, shredded
½ tablespoon flour
Freshly ground pepper
1 teaspoon salt
About ¼ teaspoon ground nutmeg
½ cup kirschwasser, cognac, or light white rum
    (optional)
2 large loaves French bread

Rub a 2-quart (or larger) chafing dish or earthenware casserole with the garlic; add the wine and heat slowly over chafing dish burner. Lightly mix the cheese with the flour; when the bubbles in the wine rise to the surface (do not boil), add cheese mixture a handful at a time, stirring until each handful melts. Continue until all cheese is melted. Add seasonings and the kirschwasser, cognac, or rum; stir well. Turn heat low but keep the fondue slowly bubbling.

Cut French bread into cubes, leaving one side of crust on each. Provide long-handled fondue forks or sturdy bamboo skewers. Each guest impales a bread cube (from soft side to crust) and dunks it into the fondue, stirring it as he does. If the fondue becomes too thick, add a little hot (never cold) wine. Serves 20.

Swiss fondue (Fondue Neufchâteloise), dipped up with French bread cubes speared on fondue forks.

Spicy Bean Cocktail Dip

This spicy-hot dip has merits beyond its remarkable flavor: it takes only minutes to blend and is inexpensive.

1 small can (8½ oz.) kidney beans, drained
1 clove garlic, minced or mashed
¼ teaspoon liquid hot-pepper seasoning
1 teaspoon Worcestershire
1 tablespoon mayonnaise
Juice of ½ lemon
½ teaspoon minced chives or finely chopped
    green onions

Put in blender the drained beans, garlic, liquid hot-pepper seasoning, Worcestershire, mayonnaise, and lemon juice. Blend until smooth, about 60 seconds (or press mixture through a wire strainer). Turn into a serving bowl and sprinkle with chives. Serve with potato wafers or thin crackers, or try it with raw carrot and celery sticks. Makes 1 cup dip.

Blocks of cream cheese make three quick, easy appetizer spreads. Coat one with toasted sesame seed, a second with chopped chives, and spoon taco sauce on third.

Bacon-Cottage Cheese Dip

You can please weight watchers if you serve this dip with vegetables instead of chips, though it's delicious with both.

16 slices bacon
1 pound sieved cottage cheese
¼ teaspoon garlic powder
Dash of cayenne
1 teaspoon onion salt
2 teaspoons lemon juice
¼ cup mayonnaise
5 teaspoons milk

Sauté bacon until crisp and brown. Crumble bacon and combine with cottage cheese, garlic powder, cayenne, onion salt, lemon juice, mayonnaise, and milk. Cover and chill. Makes about 2½ cups.

Cream Cheese Trio

Here is a simple way to use cream cheese for a triple effect. Arrange the cheese spreads on a narrow tray, and replenish taco and soy sauces as needed.

3 packages (3 oz. each) cream cheese
1 tablespoon sesame seed
1 tablespoon soy sauce (optional)
2 tablespoons chopped fresh chives
2 to 3 tablespoons taco sauce

Cream cheese should be at room temperature. Toast sesame seed by spreading them in a shallow baking pan or cooky sheet. Place in a moderate oven (350°) for about 5 minutes or until golden. Coat 1 block of cheese with sesame seed and place on tray; for added zest, drizzle soy sauce over top. Press chives into second cheese block to cover all of the surfaces generously. Place third cheese block on tray and spoon over it about half of the taco sauce; add additional sauce as required.

Curried Avocado Dip

This pre-dinner dip is zestfully seasoned with bacon, curry, and chili powder. For an added touch of color, you can top each filled avocado shell with a spoonful of red salmon caviar.

2 medium-sized avocados
4 tablespoons lemon juice
2 slices bacon, cooked until crisp, chopped
¾ teaspoon curry powder
1 clove garlic, minced or mashed
1 tablespoon minced chives
1 tablespoon mayonnaise
1 teaspoon Worcestershire
¼ teaspoon liquid hot-pepper seasoning
½ teaspoon chili powder
Salt to taste

Carefully cut the avocados in half lengthwise and remove the seeds. With a spoon remove the pulp, being sure to leave firm shells of two of the halves. Sprinkle these shells with 1 tablespoon of the lemon juice. Mash avocado pulp, add bacon and all the remaining ingredients, including the remaining lemon juice; beat until smooth. Heap the mixture into the 2 prepared shells; chill. Serve as a dip for crisp crackers, corn chips, tostadas, or small points of hot buttered rye toast. Makes about 2½ cups dip.

Favorite Cheese Spread

This cheese spread can double as a dip when it's thinned to dipping consistency with beer.

2 small packages (3 oz. each) cream cheese
4 tablespoons butter
1 teaspoon chopped capers
6 anchovy fillets, finely chopped
1 shallot or green onion without top,
    finely chopped
½ teaspoon caraway seed
1 teaspoon paprika

Allow cream cheese to soften; cream thoroughly with butter. Mix in capers, anchovies, shallot or onion, caraway seed, and paprika. Chill. Makes about 1 cup.

Chicken Liver-Cheese Dip

To save time, mix this herb-seasoned dip in your blender.

6 chicken livers, cut in small pieces
2 tablespoons butter or margarine
1 clove garlic, halved
2 tablespoons sherry
2 packages (3 oz. each) cream cheese
¼ teaspoon dried tarragon
Sour cream
Salt to taste

Sauté chicken livers in butter with the garlic until the livers are lightly browned. Remove livers and discard garlic. Add sherry to the pan, and scrape up the drippings. Into a blender container, put livers, drippings, cream cheese, tarragon, and a few tablespoons of sour cream. Blend until smooth (or press through a sieve). If necessary, add more sour cream to make a mixture of spreading or dipping consistency. Season to taste with salt. Pack into containers. Refrigerate. Makes about 1½ cups dip.

Cheese and Olive Spread

Here's an appetizer spread you can store in the freezer, ready for unexpected guests.

¼ pound Roquefort or blue cheese
¼ pound butter or margarine
1 package (3 oz.) cream cheese
2 tablespoons brandy
Dash of cayenne
¼ cup chopped walnuts
¼ cup chopped ripe olives

Blend together Roquefort, softened butter, cream cheese, brandy, cayenne, nuts, and olives. Separate mixture into 4 parts, wrap, and freeze. (If you chill the mixture first, you can shape it into rolls.) Thaw before serving with crackers. One part is adequate for 4 persons.

A giant mushroom cap, richly laden with a soft poached egg and a topping of melted cheese, makes an elegant first course serving. Recipe is on page 70.

FIRST COURSES
Impressive introductions to a meal

Caviar Mousse

This mousse is also good cut in very small cubes and placed on toast or small lettuce leaves for finger food appetizers.

1 envelope (1 tablespoon) unflavored gelatin
2 tablespoons cold water
½ cup boiling water
2 tablespoons lemon juice
2 tablespoons mayonnaise
Dash of liquid hot-pepper seasoning
4 ounces (½ cup) caviar
2 cups sour cream
Lettuce leaves

Soften gelatin in cold water. Add boiling water and stir until dissolved. Cool slightly, then stir in lemon juice, mayonnaise, liquid hot-pepper seasoning, caviar, and sour cream. Pour into shallow dish about 8 inches square. Chill until set, about 2 to 3 hours. Cut in cubes and serve on lettuce leaves. Makes 6 to 8 servings.

Oysters in Cups

If you are fortunate enough to be able to get some tiny Olympia oysters, try serving them as hors d'oeuvres in little sake cups. They are as good this way as on the half shell, and it's far easier to procure the shucked oysters.

Put 1 or 2 chilled oysters in each sake cup, place cups on a tray filled with shaved ice, and have lemon wedges (and other condiments if you wish) nearby. The guests "drink" the oysters.

Clams in Aspic

You'll need clam shells or scallop shells to make this appetizer. The velvety aspic is molded and served in the sea shell.

2 tablespoons butter
2 tablespoons flour
1 can (7 oz.) minced clams
Skim milk
Cayenne
Salt, if needed
1 tablespoon (1 envelope) unflavored gelatin
3 tablespoons water
12 clam or scallop shells
2 cans (12 oz. each) jellied madrilene

Make a roux of butter and flour. Add juice drained from clams plus enough milk to make a total of 1 cup liquid. Simmer for 10 minutes, stirring occasionally. Season to taste with cayenne and salt. Soften 1 teaspoon of the gelatin in 1 tablespoon of the water and add to hot mixture. Add clams and divide mixture into shells; chill.

Heat madrilene and stir in remaining 2 teaspoons gelatin dissolved in remaining 2 tablespoons water. Remove from heat and allow to set. Turn out aspic on heavy paper and chop. Pile on top of the clam-filled shells, and arrange remainder around as a garnish. Serve cold. Makes 12 servings.

Italian Appetizer Salad

This Italian salad somewhat combines antipasto with greens. It is perfect for a patio party.

1 small head cauliflower, broken in flowerets
1 head red lettuce
1 head escarole
1 head curly endive
1 can (1 lb.) cut green beans
1 can (1 lb.) red kidney beans
1 can (1 lb.) garbanzos
2 or 3 green onions, chopped
6 hard-cooked eggs, sliced
1 cup olive oil
½ cup-vinegar
1½ teaspoons salt
¼ teaspoon pepper
2 tomatoes, sliced
1 can (2½ oz.) sliced ripe olives
1 or 2 cans (2 oz. each) anchovies (rolled
    or fillets)

Parboil cauliflower until just slightly tender; drain. Combine in large salad bowl the greens (broken into bite-size pieces), three kinds of beans, green onions, and 4 of the eggs. Mix with dressing made with oil, vinegar, salt, and pepper. Garnish top with tomato slices, remaining egg slices, olives, and anchovies. Serve immediately. Makes 10 to 12 servings.

Avocado Bacon Cocktail

Crisp bacon gives this opening course cocktail a distinctive flavor.

¼ cup mayonnaise
½ cup chili sauce
2 tablespoons lemon juice
¼ cup orange juice
2 cups diced avocado
1 cup finely sliced celery
2 tablespoons minced chives or green onion tops
¼ cup crumbled crisp bacon

Mix together the mayonnaise, chili sauce, lemon and orange juice. Carefully fold in avocado, celery, and chives. Chill thoroughly. Serve in cocktail glasses, sprinkling the crisp bacon bits on top of each serving. Makes 6 servings.

Crab and Grapefruit Cocktail

The sharp tang of fresh grapefruit counteracts the richness of Dungeness or King crab.

3 grapefruit
½ pound crab meat (about 1 cup)
⅓ cup tomato catsup
½ teaspoon salt
¼ cup grapefruit juice
1 tablespoon Worcestershire
3 drops liquid hot-pepper seasoning
1 tablespoon finely sliced celery
¼ cup mayonnaise (optional)

Peel grapefruit with a sharp knife, removing white membrane as you peel. Slide knife blade along membrane of each segment and push the fruit out into a bowl. Drain the segments, saving the juice. Arrange alternate layers of grapefruit and crab in 8 to 10 cocktail glasses and chill.

Mix together the catsup, salt, grapefruit juice, Worcestershire, liquid hot-pepper seasoning, and celery; chill. If you like a thick cocktail sauce, blend ¼ cup mayonnaise into the catsup mixture. Spoon cocktail sauce over grapefruit and crab just before serving. If desired, garnish with lemon. Makes 8 to 10 servings.

To begin a special-occasion dinner party, have Melon with Prosciutto on the table when guests sit down.

Melon with Prosciutto

This appetizer can be served with lemon juice and black pepper in a mill for each person to grind fresh over his fruit. If you wish, you may substitute papaya for the melon.

1 ripe cantalope, cut in 6 wedges, seeds removed
6 strips prosciutto (Italian ham)
6 to 12 black olives
6 lemon wedges
Freshly ground black pepper

Cut meat of each cantalope wedge from rind, except at ends. Then cut each wedge into bites from one side, leaving opposite side uncut. Drape a strip of prosciutto over top of melon wedge. Garnish each plate with one or two black olives and a lemon wedge. Pass black pepper. Makes 6 servings.

Mushroom-stuffed Artichoke Shells

These are certain to make a hit with dinner guests.

¼ cup (⅛ lb.) butter or margarine
¼ cup dry white table wine
½ teaspoon salt
¼ teaspoon monosodium glutamate
Dash of freshly ground pepper
30 to 40 fresh small mushroom caps
    (approximately 1 pound)
10 canned or freshly cooked artichoke shells
3 tablespoons water
½ cup sour cream
Watercress sprigs for garnish

In a large frying pan, melt butter and add wine, salt, monosodium glutamate, and pepper. Add mushroom caps and simmer just until tender, stirring constantly. In an electric frying pan (or serving casserole), steam artichoke shells in the water. Stir sour cream into the mushrooms and sauce still in the first pan, and heat just until cream and sauce are blended. Spoon 3 or 4 mushrooms, along with sour cream sauce, into each artichoke shell. Serve hot with a garnish of watercress. Makes 10 appetizers.

Lime and Shrimp Cocktail

Here is a particularly refreshing cocktail sauce for shrimp and scallops.

1½ pounds deveined, shelled, and cooked
    shrimp (30 to 40 size); or poached scallops
¼ teaspoon grated lime peel
¼ cup lime juice
¼ cup dry white table wine
½ cup catsup
3 or 4 drops liquid hot-pepper seasoning
Salt and pepper to taste

Place shrimp in a deep bowl. Mix together lime peel and juice, wine, catsup, and liquid hot-pepper seasoning; pour over shrimp. Mix well and season with salt and pepper. Cover and chill well. Makes 6 servings.

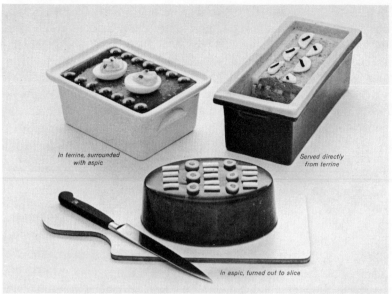

In terrine, surrounded with aspic

Served directly from terrine

In aspic, turned out to slice

Three ways to present pâtés after they are cooked and cooled. Aspic versions take extra steps, can be sliced in terrine or turned out.

HOW TO MAKE FRENCH PÂTÉ

Slices from a pâté loaf in your refrigerator make quick and elegant appetizers. Pâtés are easy to make, although the more elaborate ones take time to assemble. If properly stored, they will keep for at least a month in your refrigerator. In addition to serving them for a first course as the French do, you can serve a pâté thinly sliced on toast as appetizers, or serve slices of pâté as part of the assortment on an appetizer tray.

Ingredients for Pâté

For the basic pâté, you should have these elements ready before you begin:

Terrines. These are the dishes for baking (and usually serving) the pâté. Traditional terrines are of pottery, usually oblong or oval, with a cover. Sizes vary from 1 pint to 2 quarts. You can use a glass bread pan covered with heavy foil, or any casserole with straight enough sides for easy unmolding. Our recipe makes enough for about three 3-cup terrines.

Barding fat. This is for lining the terrines. In France the fat that comes from just under the skin on the back of the pig is used. It is difficult in this country to buy pork fat in sufficiently large pieces, but we have found that very fat salt pork can be used quite

satisfactorily. Buy a piece that weighs about 2½ pounds. This will provide enough for lining the three terrines, with some left for the *batons* (see page 67). Slice the barding fat ⅛ to ¼ inch thick and soak it (also any batons of fat) in several changes of cold water for 24 hours.

Sel Épice or Spiced Salt: For this seasoning mixture, combine 1 teaspoon ground cloves, 3 teaspoons ground nutmeg, 3 teaspoons ground ginger, 3 tablespoons ground white pepper, and ¼ cup salt. Mix well and keep tightly covered.

Basic Forcemeat: Mince 1 medium-sized onion and sauté it in 3 tablespoons butter (or rendered chicken fat) until wilted. Add ½ cup port wine, mellow sherry, or Madeira, and cook rapidly until the mixture is almost dry. Meanwhile, combine 1 pound finely ground lean raw pork, 1 pound ground pork fat, and 1 pound ground veal; mix with 3 beaten eggs, 1 teaspoon *sel épice*, 2 teaspoons salt, ½ cup whipping cream, ½ cup flour, 3 tablespoons cognac (optional), and 1 or 2 cloves garlic, pureéd. Add the onion-wine mixture and beat very well by hand, or use a heavy duty mixer. To test the seasoning, form a teaspoon of the mixture into a patty and cook in a dry frying pan, then taste. Add more spice, salt, or garlic, if you wish. This makes over 6 cups of forcemeat, or enough for three 3-cup terrines (bards, *batons*, and garnishes make up the difference).

Batons: These are the strips of meat that are arranged between layers of the forcemeat. They may be smoked tongue, ham, veal, pork fat (salt pork should be soaked as directed for barding fat), venison, rabbit, breast of duck or other game birds, chicken, or turkey. Use a combination of meats. You will need a total of about 1 pound. Cut the meat in ¼-inch strips. (Trimmings can be ground and added to the forcemeat.) Marinate for several hours in this mixture: 3 tablespoons cognac (or dry sherry), 2 tablespoons chopped shallots or green onions, and 1 teaspoon *sel épice.*

Garnishes: These are optional but elegant additions. The height of luxury is to use a *foie gras* (fat liver), cut in *batons.* However, *foie gras* is obtainable only in cans, from France, and is very expensive. Chicken livers, or the livers of duck, geese, or game, can also be used. They should be cooked, covered, in a very little stock or water, just until firm. Leave them whole if they are small, or cut them in two or three pieces if they are quite large. Truffles (available in tiny cans, from France, at fancy food stores), cut in ⅛-inch slices or ¼-inch dice, are a nice addition. Another possibility is pistachio nuts, shelled and blanched, but left whole. Marinate these garnishes in the same way as the *batons.*

Procedure for Making Pâté

Line bottom and sides of terrine with barding fat, one layer thick. Side pieces may overhang at top. Spoon in forcemeat layer, pressing it down evenly. Lay strips of meat (*batons*) on forcemeat in neat rows, alternating kinds across dish. Cover meat strips with forcemeat to fill spaces and form thin overlapping layer. Add garnishes. Repeat layers to top: forcemeat, *batons* (reverse the order in meat rows), garnishes, ending with forcemeat. Add a bay leaf and some thyme. Enclose the top forcemeat layer completely in barding fat, cover the top with a piece of heavy foil, then set on the cover of the terrine or casserole. (If you are using a bread pan, add another layer of heavy foil and fold it down over the edges.) Put the terrines into a large pan, half fill with boiling water, and bake in a moderate oven (350°) for 1 to 2 hours, depending upon the size. When done, the pâtés shrink slightly from the edges and the juices lose their pink look. Leave the terrines in the water bath, but remove the lids and weight down the meat mixture. (A good way to weight down the meat is to cover heavy cardboard with foil, or use a board or another bread pan

that is the same size; put heavy objects such as canned goods or scale weights on top.) Let stand until cool.

Once cooled, pâtés can be sliced and served directly from the baking dishes. You might want to remove the top layer of fat and decorate the top with hard-cooked egg slices and truffle strips.

Pâtés in Aspic

For an even more elegant pâté, you can surround the cooked and chilled basic pâté with aspic. It can be served directly from the terrine or turned out to slice.

To make aspic, combine 2 cans (10½ oz. each) consommé, 2 envelopes unflavored gelatin, 2 egg whites, the shells of 2 eggs, broken in bits (1 teaspoon lemon juice, and 2 tablespoons Madeira or sherry wine. Bring slowly to a boil, stirring often with a wire whip. Add 1 tablespoon cognac (optional), allow to stand for a few minutes, then put through a strainer, lined with 3 layers of wet cheesecloth. Cool.

Remove cooked pâté from dish; wash and chill dish. Pour in ¼ to ½ inch cool aspic; allow to set. Peel all fat from pâté; center pâté on firm aspic in dish, add enough cool aspic to fill the sides and to cover the top of the pâté with a ¼- to ½-inch layer. Refrigerate until firm. Use aspic-coated pâtés within 3 days.

To Keep Pâtés

Pâtés may be frozen, but they are not quite as fine in texture as those that are refrigerated. The best way to keep pâtés is to fill the terrine to the very top with rendered pork fat, cover with foil, and replace the top. Then carefully wrap the terrine in more foil.

Left, strips of meat (batons) placed on forcemeat in neat rows, alternating kinds; right, meat strips covered with forcemeat, garnishes added.

Avocado and Celery Cocktail

Butter-soft avocado contrasts with the crispness of celery in this bright-colored, well-seasoned cocktail.

4 tablespoons (¼ cup) catsup
2 tablespoons chili sauce
2 tablespoons lemon juice
½ teaspoon grated onion
¼ teaspoon prepared horseradish
Salt to taste
1 medium-sized avocado
½ cup sliced celery

Blend together catsup, chili sauce, lemon juice, onion, horseradish, and salt to taste; chill. Cut avocado in half, remove seed, peel, and cut in ½-inch cubes. Combine with celery and spoon into 4 cold cocktail glasses. Pour over the chilled sauce and serve immediately. Makes 4 servings.

Oysters Supreme

Oysters in their shells make an unusual dinner party appetizer.

6 green onions, chopped
1 bay leaf
1 tablespoon olive oil
2 jars (12 oz. each) oysters, drained and
    chopped
¼ cup dry white table wine
⅛ teaspoon crumbled dried thyme
Salt and pepper to taste
½ cup dry bread crumbs
½ cup soft bread crumbs, mixed with ¼ cup
    melted butter or margarine

Sauté onions and bay leaf in oil; add chopped oysters and cook until they stop drawing water. Pour in wine; add thyme, salt and pepper and dry crumbs. Remove bay leaf and mix well. Spoon into oyster shells. Top with buttered crumbs. Bake (and serve) shells on small foil plates, half filled with rock salt or crumpled foil, in hot over (400°) for 10 to 15 minutes, or until lightly browned. Makes 10 to 12 servings.

Special Avocado Cocktail

This avocado cocktail is topped with a rich sauce of whipped cream and caviar.

½ cup mayonnaise
½ cup cream, whipped
1 teaspoon lemon juice
2 ounces caviar
3 avocados, peeled and diced
Lettuce leaves (optional)

Make sauce by combining mayonnaise, cream, lemon juice, and caviar. Serve over diced avocado arranged in cocktail glasses. A small leaf of lettuce can garnish each serving. Makes 6 to 8 servings.

Cantaloupe Papeete

The faintly exotic aura of this melon appetizer comes from combining the bite of ginger, tang of lime, and sweetness of dates with the rich flavor of cantaloupe.

2 medium-sized chilled cantaloupes, or small
    Crenshaws or small honeydew, cut in
    halves and seeded (about 4 cups)
½ cup chopped pitted dates
1 teaspoon grated lime peel
2 tablespoons lime juice
1 tablespoon finely chopped preserved ginger
1 bottle (7 oz.) chilled ginger ale

Cut melon in balls with a ball cutter, or peel and cut in chunks. Mix with dates, lime peel and juice, and ginger. Spoon into small bowls or stemmed glasses. Pour an equal amount of ginger ale over each portion, and serve at once. Makes 8 servings.

Appetizer Cheese Cake

This handsome cheese cake appetizer is made of a well-seasoned sour cream mixture spread between top and bottom crusts of crushed cheese cracker crumbs. Because it is made well ahead of time, it is especially nice to serve if you expect to be busy on the day you entertain. You assemble the cake and then chill it for at least 24 hours until it is firm.

Melted butter or margarine
1 box (about 6 oz.) cheese crackers, finely crushed
½ cup finely chopped stuffed green olives
½ cup finely chopped celery
1 medium green pepper, finely chopped
1 small onion, finely chopped
2 tablespoons lemon juice
1 teaspoon salt
1 teaspoon Worcestershire
¼ teaspoon paprika
Dash of liquid hot-pepper seasoning
2 cups (1 pint) sour cream
Ripe olives, cut in rings
Pimiento strips
Chicory

Brush with melted butter the bottom and sides of a 9-inch spring form pan or pan with removable bottom. (You can also use a 9-inch round cake pan, or a 7 by 12-inch baking dish and serve from the dish.) Cover bottom of pan with half the crushed crackers. Mix green olives, celery, green pepper, onion, lemon juice, salt, Worcestershire, paprika, and liquid hot-pepper seasoning with sour cream; blend well. Spread sour cream mixture over cracker base. Scatter remaining half of cracker crumbs evenly over top. Cover with waxed paper and refrigerate for at least 24 hours. Remove spring form from pan; place cake (still on pan bottom) on serving platter. Garnish top with ripe olive rings and pimiento strips. Border platter with chicory. Cut in 10 or 12 wedges to serve.

Appetizer Cheese Cake with sour cream center is firm enough to cut into slender wedges for serving.

Celery Victor

This classic dish can be made ahead of time.

3 large bunches celery or 3 celery hearts
About 2½ cups chicken stock or consommé
¼ cup wine vinegar
¾ cup olive oil or salad oil
Salt and coarsely ground black pepper to taste
Shredded lettuce
2 hard-cooked eggs, chopped
12 fillets of anchovy
6 pimiento strips

Remove coarse ribs from celery stalks, split hearts lengthwise, trim off leaves, and simmer in chicken stock or consommé until tender. Drain; arrange in flat dish, and marinate in a simple French dressing made by combining wine vinegar, olive oil or salad oil, salt and pepper to taste. Chill. Serve on shredded lettuce; sprinkle with egg and garnish each half-stalk with a crossed fillet of anchovy and a strip of pimiento. Makes 6 servings.

Fettucine

This classic Italian favorite is a showpiece pasta to prepare right at the table. The making is easy, and fun to watch. You can cook the noodles as much as an hour before using and keep them warm.

3 cups hot boiled tagliarini or egg noodles
Hot water
6 tablespoons butter
1¼ cups heavy cream
1 cup shredded Parmesan cheese
Salt and pepper
Fresh grated nutmeg (or ground nutmeg)

Keep the noodles warm after cooking by floating in water that is hot to touch. In a wide frying pan or chafing dish over high heat on a range, melt butter until it is lightly browned. Add ½ cup of the cream and boil rapidly until large shiny bubbles form; stir occasionally. (You can make this part of the sauce earlier in the day, then reheat.)

Reduce heat to medium or place chafing dish over direct flame. Drain noodles well and add to the sauce. Toss vigorously with two forks, and pour in the cheese and the remaining cream, a little at a time—about three additions. The noodles should be kept moist but not too liquid. Season with salt and pepper and grate nutmeg generously over the noodles (or use about ⅛ teaspoon of the ground spice). Serve immediately. Makes 4 to 6 servings.

Fettucine with a flourish: Rapidly toss hot cooked noodles with heavy cream, cheese, and butter.

Eggs in Mushrooms

The flavors and not the ingredients make this appetizer seem rich. You may have to order ahead to get mushrooms of the proper size.

For each serving, you'll need: 1 mushroom (2½ to 3½ inches in diameter), about 1 tablespoon butter, 1 egg, salt, and about 1 tablespoon shredded Gruyère or Swiss cheese.

Carefully remove stem from each mushroom and hollow cap slightly with a small spoon. (Save scraps and stems for other uses.) In a wide frying pan, melt the butter and brown mushrooms lightly on all sides, basting them with the butter occasionally. Keep mushrooms in a warm place or over very low heat (as long as 20 to 30 minutes).

Poach eggs until whites are firm and yolks are still soft. Carefully remove eggs from cooking water and place in water that is hot to touch until you are ready to use them (you can hold them for about 30 minutes, adding more hot water as needed).

Drain eggs and place 1 in each mushroom cap; trim white if necessary to make fit. Baste with a little of the cooking butter, sprinkle with salt, and top with shredded cheese. Broil until cheese bubbles. Serve with toast points.

Tuna Appetizer Salad

This fresh appetizer salad is topped with a tuna mayonnaise.

Curly endive (chicory), or lettuce, shredded
6 or 8 thick slices peeled tomato
3 or 4 hard-cooked eggs, halved
1 cup mayonnaise
½ cup flaked tuna
1 teaspoon lemon juice
Ripe olives for garnish (optional)

On individual plates, arrange a little curly endive or shredded lettuce. On this put a thick slice of peeled tomato. Top each tomato with half a hard-cooked egg, round side up, and cover all with a tuna mayonnaise made by mixing the mayonnaise with tuna and lemon juice. Garnish each plate with ripe olives if you wish. Makes 6 or 8 servings.

Oyster-stuffed Mushrooms

For this special appetizer, you broil small oysters in large, butter-soaked mushroom caps.

24 large fresh mushroom caps
¼ cup (⅛ lb.) butter or margarine
6 green onions, finely chopped
24 small Olympia oysters
Melted butter
Salt

Sauté mushroom crowns gently in the ¼ cup butter for 3 minutes, stirring carefully so caps do not break. Remove from pan and place on greased cooky sheet, hollow side up. Sauté onions until limp in remaining butter; put about ¼ teaspoon chopped onion inside each mushroom cap. Dip oysters in melted butter; place an oyster inside each mushroom; sprinkle lightly with salt. Heat under broiler until edges of oysters start to curl. Serve at once. Makes 24 servings.

Stuffed Mushrooms

These mushroom cap appetizers, stuffed with chicken liver filling, may be served hot or cold.

1 pound large uniform mushrooms, each at least 2½ inches in diameter
¼ cup (⅛ lb.) butter or margarine
1 tablespoon minced shallots or green onion
½ pound chicken livers, finely chopped
1 small package (3 oz.) cream cheese
1 tablespoon sherry or cognac
Pinch of tarragon or dill weed
Salt and pepper to taste
Paprika or finely minced parsley for garnish

Remove mushroom stems and chop them. Cook caps in butter for 5 minutes, turning once. Remove and reserve. To same pan, add chopped stems, shallots or green onion, and chicken livers. Cook until livers begin to brown. Stir in cream cheese, sherry or cognac, tarragon or dill weed, salt, and pepper. Heap filling in caps. Serve warm, sprinkled with paprika or parsley, or chill before garnishing and serving. Makes 4 to 6 servings.

Spinach Appetizer

This appetizer goes particularly well with charcoal-broiled fish.

2 pounds spinach
3 tablespoons olive oil
¾ teaspoon salt
Pepper to taste
2 tablespoons vinegar
1 can (1 lb.) pickled beets, drained
2 hard-cooked eggs, chopped
2 lemons, quartered

Cook spinach until wilted, but still bright green. Drain and chop. Season with olive oil, salt, pepper, and vinegar. Pack into a 3 or 4-cup mold and chill for at least 2 hours. Turn out on a dish, surround with beets, and sprinkle top with chopped egg. Garnish with lemons. Makes 6 to 8 servings.

SERVE AN ANTIPASTO TRAY

Italian groceries and delicatessens carry a fascinating variety of delicacies for antipasto, the Italian appetizer course. You can choose fine salami, cheese, imported *prosciutto* ham, anchovies, black and green olives, mixed pickled vegetables (*giardiniera*), pickled small green peppers (*pepperocini*). There are no set ways to combine the flavorful foods, and that's half the fun of making up an antipasto tray.

Vegetables on the antipasto tray may be either raw or pickled. You might serve crisp celery, radishes, fennel (an Italian vegetable similar to celery), or fresh tomatoes, either plain or with olive oil and wine vinegar. Olive oil and vinegar, plus herbs and seasonings, make the marinade for the pickled vegetables that follow. These are best served in separate dishes.

Salami Antipasto Platter

A traditional antipasto combines several kinds of very thinly sliced Italian salami and sausages on a tray or platter. If you visit an Italian delicatessen, you'll find a wide variety of salami to choose from. *Galantina, mortadella, coppa sopresata* (head cheese), *zampetto*, salami *cotto, coppa veneziana* are some of the best. When melons or fresh black figs are in season, you might include on the antipasto platter paper-thin slices of *prosciutto* ham rolled around melon wedges or single figs.

Platter of Italian salami surrounded by individual dishes of raw and pickled vegetables, and Italian Appetizer Salad (recipe on page 64).

Pickled Mushrooms

1 pound whole fresh mushrooms
Boiling salted water
¼ cup wine vinegar
2 tablespoons olive oil
½ teaspoon salt
¼ teaspoon oregano
Dash pepper
1 tablespoon chopped parsley
1 small clove garlic, cut in half

Wash mushrooms and cook in a small amount of boiling salted water until just slightly tender, 5 to 10 minutes. Drain and add all remaining ingredients. Marinate in the refrigerator for several hours or longer, but remove garlic when mushrooms are flavored to taste.

Pickled Artichoke Hearts

Cook 1 package frozen artichoke hearts as directed on the package, but cook them only 3 to 5 minutes. Or use about 2 cups canned or cooked fresh artichoke hearts. Drain, and, omitting garlic, marinate as for pickled mushrooms.

Pickled Garbanzo Beans

Use 1 can (1 lb.) garbanzo beans or 2 cups cooked dried garbanzo beans. Add 2 tablespoons finely chopped onion to the ingredients for the mushroom marinade.

Pickled Cauliflower

Break apart flowerets from a small head of cauliflower. Cook until just slightly tender. Drain and marinate as for mushrooms. (You might omit the garlic and add 2 green chili peppers, chopped.)

Poached Egg Salad

The idea of a poached egg salad may seem startling, but this unusual appetizer is a very good way to begin a meal. Serve it with crisp cheese sticks.

6 eggs, very fresh with firm whites
6 slices (1 inch thick) peeled tomatoes
Lettuce leaves
Salt and pepper to taste
Chopped fresh basil
1 cup mayonnaise
¼ cup chili sauce
½ teaspoon chopped basil
2 teaspoons minced chives
2 teaspoons minced parsley

Poach eggs in rings or in a special pan. When done to your liking, lift carefully and place in cold water. Arrange each tomato slice on a nest of lettuce; sprinkle with salt, pepper, and a little chopped basil, and put a well-drained and trimmed egg on top. Mix mayonnaise with chili sauce, the ½ teaspoon basil, chives, and parsley. Pour over eggs and serve. Makes 6 servings.

Melon and Avocado Cocktail

Melon and avocado balls in a spicy tomato cocktail sauce make a refreshing first course.

1 cup avocado balls
2 tablespoons lemon juice
1 cup Persian or Crenshaw melon balls
1 cup tomato juice
1 tablespoon tomato catsup
1 teaspoon grated onion
½ teaspoon sugar
Dash of liquid hot-pepper seasoning
Salt to taste
Sprig of mint or slice of lemon for garnish
    (optional)

Roll the avocado balls in the lemon juice to prevent darkening. Add melon balls. Mix together tomato juice, catsup, onion, sugar, liquid hot-pepper seasoning, and salt. Pour over avocado and melon balls and chill thoroughly. Spoon into chilled glasses. If desired, garnish with a sprig of mint or a slice of lemon. Makes 4 servings.

Tomato wedges, grapefruit segments, and shrimp make a colorful and refreshing first course for dinner.

Tomato Seafood Cocktail

This tomato-seafood combination looks attractive in stemmed cocktail glasses.

Tiny spears crisp romaine lettuce
3 firm tomatoes, peeled and cut into wedges
1 large grapefruit, peeled and cut into segments
½ pound medium-sized shrimp, peeled and
    cooked, or crab legs or lobster meat
1 cup catsup
⅓ cup dry white table wine
3 tablespoons wine vinegar
1 tablespoon grated onion
2 teaspoons prepared horseradish
Dash of liquid hot-pepper seasoning

Line cocktail glasses with tiny spears of crisp romaine. Arrange tomato wedges, grapefruit segments, and shrimp over romaine. Top with dressing made by blending catsup, wine, wine vinegar, onion, horseradish, and a dash of liquid hot-pepper seasoning. Chill for 1 hour or more. Makes about 1½ cups dressing, enough for 6 servings.

To make pickled Smelt Rolls: Lift bone from smelt with your fingers after cleaning fish; roll up with onion filling; chill in marinade for 12 hours; serve on lettuce.

Ceviche Buena Vista

Ceviche, a popular appetizer in Mexico, is raw fish "cooked" in lime or lemon juice. Dolphinfish is the base of this recipe.

¾ pound dolphinfish (mahimahi), skinned and
    boned if necessary
½ cup lime juice or lemon juice
About ¼ teaspoon salt
2 teaspoons soy sauce
2 teaspoons sugar
1 tablespoon minced onion
Salt to taste
Several slices lime
Juice of 1 lime

Cut fish in ½-inch cubes and place in a small, deep bowl. Mix the ½ cup lime juice with ¼ teaspoon salt, soy sauce, and sugar. Pour over fish, cover, and chill for at least 6 hours. Drain. Mix fish with onion and salt to taste; put in serving dish. Garnish with lime slices. Pour lime juice over fish. Spear cubes with small skewers and eat alone, or on crackers. Makes about 6 servings.

Smelt Rolls

Serve these delicious pickled fish as the Scandinavians do, with thin rye crackers.

1 pound small smelt (12 to 16 per pound)
1 medium-sized onion, finely chopped
2 teaspoons salt
¼ teaspoon pepper
1 teaspoon dill weed
½ cup white wine vinegar or regular
    white vinegar
½ cup dry white wine or water
1 teaspoon sugar

Cut off heads and tails of smelt, clean, and cut each from end to end with scissors. Then lift out bone from each smelt with fingers (unless you have bought boneless smelt). Combine onion, salt, pepper, and dill weed. Spread on the flesh side of each piece of smelt. Start at head end of boned smelt and roll up to enclose filling. Arrange rolls, with open ends down, in an ungreased 1½-quart casserole. Pour over a mixture of vinegar, wine, and sugar. Cover and bake in moderate oven (350°) for 15 to 20 minutes. Cool in liquid, and chill for at least 12 hours. (You can keep pickled smelt in the refrigerator up to 2 weeks.) Serve on lettuce to eat with fork. Makes 6 to 8 servings of 2 rolls each.

Caponata

This dish originated on the island of Sicily. It combines the mild but distinctive flavor of eggplant with the smoothness of olive oil and the tartness of olives, capers, and vinegar. Serve it as a first course mounded on a bed of greens and accompanied by crisp crackers or crusty Italian or French bread. Caponata is best when made at least a day before serving so the various flavors have time to blend. It keeps well; cover it tightly and store it in your refrigerator for as long as a week.

½ cup olive oil
2 cups diced celery
1 medium-sized unpeeled eggplant, cut in
    ¾-inch cubes
1 large onion, chopped
⅓ cup wine vinegar
1 teaspoon sugar
2 large tomatoes, peeled and diced
1 cup water
1 tablespoon capers, drained
¼ cup sliced pimiento-stuffed green olives
1 can (2¼ oz.) sliced black olives, drained
2 tablespoons minced parsley
Salt to taste

Heat the olive oil in a large frying pan; add the celery and cook, stirring often, until tender (about 7 minutes). Remove celery from pan with a slotted spoon and set aside.

Add eggplant to pan and cook over medium heat, stirring, until it is lightly browned and tender (about 10 minutes). Add the onion and continue cooking and stirring until the onion is soft but not browned. Using a slotted spoon, lift the eggplant and onion out of the pan and set aside.

Add to the pan the vinegar, sugar, tomatoes, and water; cook over medium heat, stirring, until a fairly smooth sauce is formed (about 5 minutes).

Return the celery, eggplant, and onion to the pan with the sauce. Stir in the capers, olives, and parsley and simmer about 20 minutes longer. Taste and add salt if needed. Remove from heat, cool, and chill until needed. Caponata is best served at room temperature, so remove it from the refrigerator about 20 minutes before you plan to serve it. Makes 6 to 8 servings.

Serve Artichokes Vinaigrette well chilled and topped with bits of pimiento, parsley, pickles from marinade.

Artichokes Vinaigrette

Tiny artichokes marinated in a tart, faintly sweet dressing with bits of pimiento, pickle, and parsley, are colorful and refreshing.

1 package (9 oz.) frozen artichoke hearts or
    2 cups fresh trimmed and halved artichoke
    hearts
6 tablespoons olive oil
2 tablespoons red wine vinegar
3 tablespoons minced sweet pickle
1 tablespoon sweet pickle liquid
2 tablespoons minced parsley
2 tablespoons minced pimiento

Cook artichokes in boiling salted water as directed on the package, or cook fresh artichoke hearts until tender. Drain and place in a small deep bowl. Pour over them the olive oil and vinegar. Gently mix in pickle, pickle liquid, parsley, and pimiento. Cover and chill for at least 4 hours or overnight. Lift artichokes from marinade and arrange 6 to 8 halves on each individual plate. With a slotted spoon, remove some of the chopped ingredients from marinade and spoon over artichokes. Makes 4 servings.

BEVERAGES
Refreshing punches, milk drinks, juices

Champagne Punch

Strawberries garnish this refreshing punch, made with grapefruit soda, sauterne, and champagne.

1 bottle (4/5 qt.) sauterne, well chilled
1 bottle (4/5 qt.) champagne, chilled
2 bottles (1 qt. each) grapefruit soda, well chilled
2 cups washed, stemmed strawberries

In a punch bowl, mix together until blended the sauterne, champagne, and grapefruit soda. Drop in strawberries. Ladle some of the punch into each punch glass or champagne glass, and add a strawberry to each serving. Makes about 18 to 20 six-ounce servings.

Muscat Wine Punch

Appetizers and muscat wine punch make an elegant first course for a buffet dinner.

3 bottles (4/5 qt. each) Riesling, well chilled
1 bottle (4/5 qt.) black muscat, well chilled
2 bottles (1 qt. each) sparkling water, well chilled
2 cups muscat grapes, washed and stemmed, or a small cluster of muscat grapes

Blend the chilled wines and sparkling water in a punch bowl. Add muscat grapes. Ladle the punch into wine glasses, adding a few grapes to each serving. From an ice bucket, add a piece of ice to keep each drink chilled. Makes 12 to 14 servings.

Cider Wassail Bowl

This version of hot and spicy English wassail has the traditional roasted apples bobbing on top.

3 tablespoons light corn syrup
3 tablespoons sugar
¼ teaspoon cinnamon
8 lady apples or 5 small red cooking apples, washed and dried
2 quarts apple cider
1 whole lemon, thinly sliced
1 cinnamon stick
4 whole cloves

Heat corn syrup in a small pan; combine sugar with the ¼ teaspoon cinnamon on a shallow dish. Roll each apple in hot syrup, then in the sugar; arrange in a baking pan, and bake in a hot oven (400°) until partially cooked, about 15 minutes (apples should not lose their shape).

In a large pan, heat slowly over very low heat to just below boiling point the apple cider, lemon, cinnamon stick, and cloves. Before serving, strain out the spices and add the roasted apples. Serve piping hot. The lady apples may be served with the punch. Makes 12 six-ounce servings.

Three ways to serve horchata (page 87) as an unusual and refreshing summer drink: Cantaloupe Horchata with cinnamon stick, Horchata Curaçao with lemon, Mexican Almond Horchata with orange blossoms.

May Wine Punch

Serve this sparkling red wine punch with a few strawberries in each glass.

½ cup fresh sweet woodruff
2 bottles Riesling (4/5 qt. each)
1 bottle Burgundy (4/5 qt.)
5 tablespoons sugar
2 cups whole strawberries
1 quart ginger ale, chilled
⅓ cup orange juice

Wash the woodruff leaves and blossoms and steep in the Riesling and red wine at room temperature for 45 minutes to 1 hour. Add 2 tablespoons of the sugar; stir until dissolved. Mix the strawberries with the remaining 3 tablespoons sugar; put in a chilled punch bowl. Strain wine mixture into the bowl, and add ginger ale and orange juice. Pack bowl in chopped ice. (Do not add ice to punch.) Makes 12 to 16 servings.

Hot Cider Punch

You'll need a serving container that can be placed over a flame or on a hot tray for this cider punch.

3 quarts cider or apple juice
2 to 3 quarts sauterne (or substitute with more cider)
12 cloves
4 cinnamon sticks
Orange slices for garnish

Mix the cider, sauterne, cloves, and cinnamon sticks in a large kettle; leave at least 30 minutes. Immediately before serving, heat just until hot. Garnish with orange slices. Makes 18 servings.

Mock Champagne

Mock champagne is a good beverage to serve family groups.

½ cup sugar
½ cup water
½ cup grapefruit juice
¼ cup orange juice
2 cups ginger ale (chilled)
3 tablespoons grenadine syrup
Lemon peel

Combine sugar and water in a saucepan; boil slowly for 10 minutes, stirring only until sugar is dissolved; cool. Mix sugar syrup, grapefruit juice, and orange juice; chill thoroughly. Just before serving, add ginger ale and grenadine. Serve in champagne or sherbet glasses and put a twist of lemon peel in each glass. Makes 5 or 6 servings.

Swedish Punch

You can make this spiced fruit punch a day ahead and heat it just before serving.

2½ cups cranberry juice cocktail
Brown sugar or raw sugar to taste (optional)
2 cinnamon sticks, each about 3 inches long
6 whole cardamom, pods crushed open
⅛ teaspoon ground allspice
1 tablespoon butter
Grapefruit wedges
Whole cloves

Combine cranberry juice cocktail, brown sugar or raw sugar to taste (if desired), cinnamon sticks, cardamom, and ground allspice. At this point you can let the punch stand overnight to give flavors time to blend more thoroughly.

Bring to a boil; let simmer 5 minutes. Strain. Add butter, stirring until melted. Pour into serving cups, and decorate rims of the cups with wedges of grapefruit, each studded with several whole cloves. Makes 5 or 6 servings.

Cranberry Special

The natural tang of both cranberry and grapefruit juices makes this beverage particularly tart.

3 cups sugar
2 bottles (1 pint each) cranberry juice cocktail
2 quarts grapefruit or pineapple juice (1 large 46-oz. can and 1 medium-sized 1 lb., 4 oz. can)
4 quarts ginger ale

Stir sugar into cranberry juice until dissolved. Add grapefruit or pineapple juice and chill. Pour into a punch bowl and stir in ginger ale just before serving. Makes about 50 to 60 servings.

Holiday Wine Punch

When you need punch for a large group, try this, over ice, in a massive bowl.

3 cans (6 oz. each) frozen pineapple juice concentrate
3 cans (6 oz. each) frozen orange juice concentrate
2 cans (6 oz. each) frozen concentrate for lemonade or limeade
½ cup white corn syrup
1 bottle (1/5 gal.) muscatel, sherry, or white port wine
3 quarts cold water
2 quarts sparkling water or ginger ale

Combine the 3 fruit juice concentrates, corn syrup, and wine. Mix well and refrigerate for several hours, or overnight, to blend flavors. Pour chilled liquids into the punch bowl over a block of ice (or add ice cubes); add water and sparkling water. Blend. Makes about 3 gallons.

A cooling punch for a reception or large party: Ginger Wine Punch garnished with mint sprigs and lemon.

Ginger Wine Punch

Lemon slices and sprigs of mint float on the top of this light amber, sparkling punch. It shows off best in a clear glass bowl.

2 bottles (1 qt. each) ginger ale, chilled
3 bottles (4/5 qt. each) sauterne, chilled
3 sprigs mint
1 whole lemon, thinly sliced

In a large punch bowl, mix together the chilled ginger ale and chilled wine. Place mint sprigs and lemon slices on the top for garnish. Add a chunk of ice to keep punch chilled. Serve in punch cups. Makes about 22 to 24 six-ounce servings.

Julglögg (Christmas Wine)

In Scandinavian communities, glögg (pronounced glug) is well known. It is the traditional hot Christmas wine of Sweden.

10 whole cardamom
5 whole cloves
1 stick cinnamon
1 cup whole blanched almonds
1 cup raisins
4 dried figs
Peel from 3 oranges, cut in long strips
2 bottles (4/5 qt.) dry white wine
1 bottle (4/5 qt.) dry red wine
½ cup sugar

In a pan, combine cardamom, cloves, cinnamon, almonds, raisins, and figs. Add orange peel to the pan with 1 bottle of the dry white wine. Cover and heat slowly just to the boiling point. Cool, cover, and store until time to serve—at least 2 days.

Before serving, remove the figs, orange peel, and whole spices, leaving raisins and almonds in the wine. Add the other bottle of dry white wine, the dry red wine, and sugar; heat, but do not boil. Serve hot with some of the raisins and almonds in each wine glass or punch cup (preheat glasses in hot water). Makes about 15 six-ounce servings.

If you wish to flame the punch, omit sugar in the recipe; arrange 1 cup sugar cubes on a cake rack or flat grater, suspended over the punch. Heat ½ to 1 cup aquavit, brandy, or rum; pour half of it over the sugar cubes. Light remaining aquavit and pour flaming over the sugar (at least half the sugar should melt into the punch).

Sangria

This popular Spanish punch is made with red wine, orange juice, lemon juice, and sparkling water.

1 whole orange
1 whole lemon, thinly sliced
Juice of 1 lemon
2 bottles (4/5 qt. each) Burgundy or Pinot Noir
½ cup sugar
1 bottle (1 qt.) sparkling water, chilled

Cut the outer ring from the orange in a spiral strip, removing as little of the white membrane as possible. Then squeeze orange juice. In a large bowl, mix together the orange spiral, orange juice, lemon slices, and lemon juice. Add the Burgundy and sugar. Stir until the sugar is dissolved. Chill at least 4 hours. Remove the lemon slices and orange peel. Pour into a punch bowl; add sparkling water. Makes 12 to 14 servings.

Wine Syllabub

This punch with a frothy top is a near-cousin to eggnog, but with a light taste of wine and lemon.

1 cup sugar
1 bottle (4/5 qt.) dry white wine
3 tablespoons finely grated lemon peel
⅓ cup lemon juice
3 cups cold milk
2 cups (1 pt.) light cream
4 egg whites
Nutmeg

Combine ½ cup of the sugar with wine, lemon peel, and lemon juice. Stir until the sugar is completely dissolved; chill well. In your punch bowl, blend milk and light cream. Pour in the wine mixture and beat with a rotary beater or wire whip until frothy. Beat egg whites until firm; gradually add the remaining ½ cup sugar, beating until stiff and glossy. Put spoonful puffs of this meringue on top of punch. Sprinkle lightly with nutmeg. Makes about 18 half-cup servings.

Large fish bowl is ideal for serving clear White Wine Punch with colorful fruits. Add a string of shiny balls around rim and drop in some colored glass floats.

Double-boiler Mulled Wine

Serve this wine in mugs and garnish each serving with a sliced lemon round.

1 cinnamon stick, 2 inches long
1 teaspoon whole cloves
⅛ of a whole nutmeg
3 tablespoons lemon juice
½ cup sugar
1 bottle (4/5 qt.) dry red wine (Burgundy, zinfandel)
1½ cups port
Sliced lemon rounds

Rub the cinnamon stick with a grater, or use a mortar and pestle until it is well broken up. Grind the cloves and nutmeg in a nutmeg grinder. Place the spices in the top of a double boiler with the lemon juice, sugar, red wine, and port. Place over hot water and heat for 20 minutes, or until sugar is thoroughly dissolved and spice flavor has permeated the mixture. Place a lemon round in each mug or cup and ladle the mulled wine into the cups. Makes 8 servings.

White Wine Punch

This light wine punch with pieces of fruit shows off best in a clear glass bowl. Have all ingredients well chilled.

2 bottles (4/5 qt. each) dry white wine
2 quarts apple juice
6 tablespoons lemon juice
1 small can (14 oz.) pineapple chunks
1 jar (8 oz.) maraschino cherries
1 small bunch grapes
Chunk of ice

In your punch bowl, combine wine, apple juice, and lemon juice. Drain pineapple chunks and maraschino cherries; drop into the punch along with grapes. Add chunk of ice to keep punch chilled. Serve some fruit in each cup. Makes about 25 six-ounce servings.

Minted Amber Punch

Fresh mint, which you steep in syrup, adds a refreshing quality to this golden punch. You may use the handy canned or frozen citrus and pineapple juices.

30 sprigs fresh mint, washed
2 cups sugar
2 quarts boiling water
2 cups lemon juice
8 cups orange juice
2 cups pineapple juice
2 quarts ginger ale

Place mint sprigs in a large saucepan. Add sugar and boiling water and simmer for 15 minutes. Chill. Strain and combine with the chilled lemon, orange, and pineapple juices, and ginger ale. Makes about 50 servings.

Sparkling Cranberry Punch

Use either ginger ale or champagne for the sparkle in this clear, red punch.

3 bottles (1 pt. each) cranberry juice cocktail
2 cups orange juice
¼ cup lemon juice
2 quart bottles ginger ale, or 2 bottles (4/5 qt. each) champagne

Combine cranberry juice with orange juice and lemon juice; chill well. Just before serving, pour into your punch bowl and add ginger ale or champagne. Serve in punch cups or champagne glasses. Makes about 20 six-ounce servings.

Buttered Cranberry Punch

Serve this bright red punch piping hot in mugs, with cinnamon sticks for stirrers.

½ to ¾ cup brown sugar, firmly packed
¼ teaspoon salt
¼ teaspoon nutmeg
½ teaspoon cinnamon
½ teaspoon allspice
¾ teaspoon ground cloves
4 cups water
2 cans (1 lb. each) jellied cranberry sauce
1 quart canned pineapple juice
Butter or margarine
Whole cinnamon sticks (optional)

Mix the sugar and spices with 1 cup of the water and bring to a boil. In a large pan, crush cranberry sauce with a fork; add remaining 3 cups water, and beat until smooth. Add pineapple juice and the spiced syrup; simmer about 5 minutes. Serve hot, topped with a dot of butter, and add cinnamon stick for stirrers if you wish. Makes 2½ quarts, 20 servings.

Chili-Tomato Cocktail

Canned chilies work nicely in this chili-tomato cocktail.

2 green chilies, peeled
1 can (12 oz.) tomato juice
¼ teaspoon salt
2 lemon wedges

Rinse seeds from green chilies and put them in a blender with tomato juice and salt. Blend smooth and chill before serving with a wedge of lemon. If you have no blender, force the chilies through a food mill, then add to the tomato juice and mix well. Makes 2 servings.

Lemon-Lime Tomato Juice

This tangy tomato juice cocktail goes well with an assortment of crisp vegetables. Ingredients should chill several hours before time to serve.

¼ cup lemon juice
¼ cup lime juice
1 tray ice cubes
1 large can (32 oz.) tomato juice, chilled
2 cans (12 oz. each) lemon-lime flavored soda, chilled
Thin slices of lime for garnish

Combine lemon juice and lime juice in a large pitcher or bowl. Just before serving, add ice cubes to the mixture. Then pour in tomato juice and lemon-lime flavored soda. Garnish with thin slices of lime. Makes about 10 cups.

Hot Tomato Juice Cocktail

Make this cocktail early in the day and heat it just before dinner.

3 cups tomato juice
3 whole cloves
1 tablespoon lemon juice
1½ teaspoons sugar
1½ teaspoons salt
Dash of black pepper
¾ cup dry white wine (optional)

Combine tomato juice, cloves, lemon juice, sugar, salt, dash black pepper, and wine if desired. Just before serving, heat, but do not boil. Makes 6 servings.

Milk Punch

Here is a good appetizer for a brunch. Prepare milk punch quickly in a blender.

1 cup brandy
2 cups cold milk
6 tablespoons powdered sugar
½ teaspoon vanilla
6 to 8 ice cubes, coarsely crushed
Nutmeg

Pour brandy into blender with milk, sugar, vanilla, and ice cubes. Whirl the mixture until it is frothy and well blended. Pour into glasses or punch cups, and sprinkle with nutmeg. Makes about 5½ cups punch.

Orange Buttermilk

You need not be a fan of buttermilk to enjoy this smooth thick drink, for the buttermilk flavor is unidentifiable.

½ can (6 oz. size) frozen concentrated orange
    juice (tangerine, orange-banana, or
    pineapple frozen concentrated juice
    may also be used)
2 cups churned buttermilk

Partially thaw orange juice. In pitcher, blend with buttermilk. Serve over ice. Makes 2 large glasses.

Refreshing drink whirled in blender: fresh pineapple, ripe banana, and buttermilk. Serve chilled, over ice.

Pineapple Buttermilk

Fresh pineapple and ripe banana are whirled in a blender with buttermilk to make this refreshing drink.

1⅓ cups churned buttermilk
½ ripe banana
⅔ cup diced fresh pineapple mixed with 1 table-
    spoon sugar, or ⅔ cup canned crushed pine-
    apple.

Pour buttermilk into an electric blender. Add banana and pineapple. Whirl until smooth. Chill in refrigerator or serve over ice. Makes 2 large glasses.

Breakfast Peach Punch

Put the peaches in the refrigerator the night before so this nutritious peach eggnog will be cold.

2 fully-ripe, medium-sized peaches, chilled, peeled, and pitted
2 eggs
2 tablespoons thawed frozen orange juice concentrate
½ cup milk

Combine peaches with eggs, orange juice concentrate, and milk. Whirl in a blender until smooth, or slice peach and mix all with an electric beater until fairly smooth. Makes 2 servings.

Frothy Eggnog Punch

You can prepare this eggnog punch several hours in advance.

14 eggs, separated
1¼ cups sugar
1 quart milk
1 cup (½ pint) whipping cream
1 cup (½ pint) light rum
1 cup (½ pint) brandy

Beat egg yolks until smooth. Combine with ¾ cup of the sugar and ¾ cup of the milk in a large saucepan; place over medium-low heat; cook, stirring until it thickens to a soft custard (about 12 minutes); cool. Beat egg whites until frothy; add remaining ½ cup sugar and beat until they form soft peaks; spoon into cooled custard. Whip the cream in the same bowl. Add whipped cream and remaining 3¼ cups milk to beaten whites and custard; gently mix together. Refrigerate for several hours or overnight. Just before pouring into punch bowl, stir in the rum and brandy. Makes 15 to 20 servings.

Lemon and Orange Frostie

If you keep one ice tray filled with grenadine flavored cubes of fruit juice, you can serve this festive beverage at a minute's notice.

1 cup water
1 cup sugar
1 cup unstrained orange juice
1 cup lemon juice
2 tablespoons grenadine syrup
1 large bottle ginger ale, chilled

Combine water, sugar, orange juice, lemon juice, and grenadine in a pitcher; stir until sugar is dissolved; pour into refrigerator ice cube tray and freeze. To serve, place 3 or 4 frozen cubes in each tall glass, crush slightly with a fork (because of sugar, cubes will be soft), then fill glass with chilled ginger ale. Makes enough for 6 glasses.

Orange Sherry Cocktail

Prepare 2 small (6 oz. each) cans frozen orange juice concentrate as directed on the can. Stir in 2 cups sherry (or ginger ale); chill. Makes 12 to 16 small servings.

Golden Punch

This cantaloupe-colored punch is one of the simplest of all to prepare. Its full, rich flavor can stand diluting, slightly, with decorative ice cubes or an ice block.

2 cans (6 oz. each) frozen orange juice concentrate
2 cans (6 oz. each) frozen lemonade concentrate
2 cans (12 oz. each) apricot nectar
2 cans (1 pt., 2 oz. each) pineapple juice

Add water to frozen concentrates as directed on the cans. Combine with the apricot nectar and pineapple juice. Chill. Makes 6 quarts or about 50 servings.

TIPS ON MAKING PUNCH

A good punch, with a cool look and a refreshing flavor, is the easiest possible beverage to serve to a large group. Here are a number of ways to make your punch outstanding.

For a clearer punch, strain all fruit juices before blending.

Tea makes a good punch base and combines well with all fruit juices. It makes a darker colored punch with more "body" than water.

For less sweet punches, use dry ginger ale and plain sparkling water.

Dry white table wines, such as chablis, sauterne, or the Rieslings, blend well with fruit juices and make a refreshing punch.

Mix all ingredients, except carbonated beverages, and refrigerate 24 hours to blend the flavors and give a "mellow" quality to the punch.

Refrigerate all ingredients until thoroughly chilled before adding the ice. You should not depend on an ice garnish to chill punch—the punch takes too long to cool and the decorative ice block or cubes melt too fast.

Ice blocks or cubes made with fruit juice or ginger ale instead of water do not thin the punch on melting. (However, they don't look as crystal clear as regular ice.)

Place the ice garnish in the punch bowl at the last minute.

Ways to Decorate the Punch

These garnishes, added to the punch bowl just before your guests arrive, will give your party table a festive look.

Party ice cubes: Fill ice cube trays about ⅔ full with water, ginger ale, or fruit juices; freeze. Then place maraschino cherries with stems, mint sprigs, pineapple cubes, or lime wedges on ice and pour in enough more liquid to cover. Finish freezing.

Floating islands: Scoop balls of orange, lemon, lime, pineapple, or raspberry sherbet. Freeze firm. Drop into filled punch bowl just before serving. (You might stick a tiny sprig of mint on top of each sherbet ball.)

Flowers: Float gardenias, camellias, or other suitable flowers in the punch bowl. Select small, perfect flowers. Wash stems and leaves. Float directly on the surface of punch or place on the ice block. (Wedding punches sometimes have small clusters of lilies-of-the-valley, tied with white satin ribbon, laid on the center of the ice block.)

Flavorful stirrers: Use whole cinnamon sticks or thin lemon, lime, mint, or orange candy sticks as "stirrers" for individual servings.

Fruit floaters: With a toothpick, skewer small whole berries on each side of a fairly thick slice of lime or lemon and float in the punch bowl.

Christmas "holly" wreath: Pour about ¾ inch of water in a ring mold; freeze. When solid, arrange a wreath of leaves (mint, ivy, holly, or any attractive dark green leaves) around it, undersides facing up. Put cherries in strategic spots around the wreath. Carefully pour in ¼ inch of water and freeze again. Fill the ring mold with water and freeze again. Just before the well-iced punch is served, unmold the wreath of ice and float it on top of the bowl.

Dry ice: With a little care, you can use dry ice in a punch bowl for an exotic effect. The fog of carbon dioxide that comes bubbling off is tasteless and harmless. However, dry ice is much colder than regular ice, and too much added at once can freeze the punch and break the bowl. (Because it is so very cold, it is also dangerous to swallow a piece of it.) Crack the dry ice into large chunks and put about a cupful at a time into the punch bowl. Keep the rest in a metal container and handle it with tongs.

Papaya-Mandarina Sorbete

A pastel colored drink made of fruit juice and milk, known as "sorbete," is a favorite appetizer in many South American countries. This sorbete has a particularly pretty orange color.

1 fresh papaya, peeled and seeded
1 banana, peeled
1 can (11 oz.) mandarin oranges, including
    syrup
2 tablespoons sugar
½ cup milk

In a blender container, put the papaya, banana, mandarin oranges and syrup, and sugar; blend thoroughly. Add milk; blend about ½ minute more. Chill. Makes about 4 servings.

Sorbetes are delicious combinations of fruit juices and fruit pulps, blended with milk and served chilled.

Guava Sorbete

Here is a subtly flavored, pale mauve sorbete.

1 can (12 oz.) guava nectar, or 1 cup fresh
    guava pulp
½ banana
3 teaspoons sugar
1 teaspoon lemon juice
½ cup milk

Blend together thoroughly guava nectar, banana, sugar, and lemon juice. Add milk; blend. Chill. Makes about 4 servings.

Strawberry-Banana Sorbete

Strawberries and banana combine to make this unusually flavored sorbete.

1 cup whole strawberries
1 banana
2 teaspoons sugar
½ cup milk

Blend strawberries, banana, and sugar. Add milk and blend. Chill. Makes about 4 servings.

Berry Sorbete

This deep purple sorbete is very popular in South America.

1 cup whole fresh strawberries
½ cup canned blackberry nectar
2 tablespoons sugar
1 cup milk

Blend together strawberries, blackberry nectar, and sugar. Add milk and blend. Chill. Makes about 4 servings.

Horchata Curaçao

This is a version of the light, cool, slightly sweet drinks called by the Spanish name "horchata." It uses sweet almonds with a small amount of almond extract to heighten the oil of almond flavor.

2 cups blanched almonds
¾ cup sugar
4 cups water
1¼ teaspoons almond extract
Few grains salt
6 thin lemon slices

Put the almonds through the fine blade of your food chopper or whirl in your blender until finely ground. Combine sugar and water in a pan and boil until the sugar is dissolved. Pour over the almonds and let stand at room temperature for 1 hour. Strain through 4 thicknesses of cheesecloth, squeezing the cloth to extract all the liquid; discard nuts. Stir in almond extract and salt, and chill thoroughly. Stir again before serving; pour over ice, and garnish each glass with a lemon slice. Let each person squeeze a little lemon juice into his drink to provide a delicate citrus accent. Makes 6 servings.

Mexican Almond Horchata (Horchata de Almendras)

This horchata has flowery overtones contributed by orange blossom water and cherry brandy. An attractive way to serve it is in wide, shallow-bowled champagne glasses. Float a washed orange or lemon blossom or other fragrant blossom in each glass.

4½ cups water
9 tablespoons sugar
1½ cups blanched almonds, finely ground
1 tablespoon orange flower water
1 tablespoon kirsch (cherry brandy)
6 washed fragrant blossoms

Boil the water and sugar together until the sugar is dissolved. Pour over the ground almonds and allow to stand at room temperature for 1 hour. Strain through 4 thicknesses of cheesecloth, squeezing out all the liquid; discard nuts. Stir in the orange blossom water and kirsch, cover, and chill for 8 hours or more. Stir before serving. Pour over ice in glasses, and garnish each with a flower blossom. Makes 6 servings.

Cantaloupe Horchata

The most common horchata in Mexico is made with cantaloupe seeds, but you can also use the seeds of any other melon—Crenshaw, casaba, honeydew, even watermelon. You taste a delicate but definite fruity flavor of the melon in this drink, which is spiced very lightly with cinnamon.

4 cups water
¾ cup sugar
2 cups cantaloupe seeds, rinsed and finely ground
Few grains salt
Dash ground cinnamon
6 whole cinnamon sticks

Boil the water and sugar together until sugar is dissolved. Pour over the ground seeds, and let stand at room temperature for 1 hour. Strain through 4 thicknesses of cheesecloth, squeezing to extract all the liquid; discard seeds. Stir in the salt and cinnamon. Cover and chill thoroughly. Stir before serving. Pour into ice-filled glasses and garnish each serving with a cinnamon stick. Makes 6 servings.

Decorative foods for an afternoon tea: tiny sandwiches with leaves and flowers. Sandwiches, left to right: Watercress Cream Cheese, Nasturtium Blossom, Cucumber Dill, Rose Petal Honey, Chinese Parsley Ginger. Recipes, pages 89, 94, 95.

PARTY SANDWICHES

Delectable bites for teas and receptions

Chinese Parsley Ginger Sandwiches

The exotic flavors of Chinese parsley and ginger combine in these rolled sandwiches.

15 slices white bread, ¼ inch thick
½ cup (¼ pound) soft butter
2 tablespoons minced crystallized or preserved ginger
About ¼ cup Chinese parsley leaves (if unavailable, add ½ teaspoon ground coriander to butter mixture and sprinkle sandwiches with a little minced parsley)

Trim crusts off bread slices. Blend butter with ginger and spread evenly on one side of each slice of bread. Scatter Chinese parsley leaves over surface. Roll each slice rather compactly as for a jelly roll; wrap in waxed paper and chill until sandwiches hold shape, about 1½ hours. Makes 15.

Rose Petal Honey Sandwiches

Here are decorative little tea sandwiches with the perfume of roses.

½ cup (¼ pound) soft butter
4 teaspoons honey
¼ cup washed and drained minced rose petals (use clean, *unsprayed* roses with a good fragrance)
10 or 12 slices white bread, ¼ inch thick

Blend butter with honey and minced rose petals. Spread mixture on half the bread slices; top with remaining bread slices. Cut into squares, rounds, or diamonds, trimming off crust. Each sandwich will make 2 or 3 small sandwiches; total will be 10 to 18.

Watercress Cream Cheese Sandwiches

To be at their best, these should be prepared within a few hours of serving.

Trim crust from ¼-inch slices of firm-textured rye bread. Cut in half rounds or rectangles. Spread each generously with soft cream cheese and top with watercress leaves.

Currant-Mint Rolls

These dainty sandwiches are a good choice for a tea or wedding reception.

2 pounds soft butter or margarine
2 cups red currant jelly
1 cup finely chopped fresh mint
1 teaspoon seasoned salt
¼ cup lemon juice
About 100 sandwich bread slices, crusts trimmed
Soft butter or margarine
100 mint sprigs (optional)

Beat the butter until soft; beat jelly until almost smooth. Combine butter, jelly, mint, seasoned salt, and lemon juice; mix well. Roll each bread slice lightly with the rolling pin; spread with butter. Spread filling on bread; roll up like a jelly roll; fasten with a toothpick. Cover with a damp cloth and chill. Just before serving tuck a tiny sprig of mint into one end of each if you wish. Makes 100.

Crab Salad Sandwich

A miniature salad tops this tiny open face sand-wich.

2 quarts crab meat (or use cooked and chopped
    lobster or shrimp)
1 pint finely chopped celery
½ cup mayonnaise
¼ cup chili sauce
¼ cup lime juice or lemon juice
½ cup finely chopped green onion or chives
6 hard-cooked eggs, chopped (optional)
Seasoned salt to taste
About 50 sandwich bread slices, trimmed
About ¾ cup soft butter
100 tiny lettuce cups or spears (butter lettuce
    or romaine)

Combine the crab meat, celery, mayonnaise, chili sauce, lime juice, green onion, hard-cooked eggs (if used), and seasoned salt. Chill until ready to use. Cut each bread slice into 2 rounds or squares; spread each with butter. Just before serving, top each piece of bread with a tiny lettuce cup, romaine spear, or shredded lettuce. Spoon in a small mound of the crab salad. Makes 100.

Savory Butter Spread

The following butter spread not only prevents moist fillings from soaking into bread, but adds mild extra flavor that blends well with almost any filling except a sweet or fruit one.

Soften 2 pounds butter or margarine (or one pound of each) and blend in 1 teaspoon dill weed or rosemary and ¼ cup finely chopped parsley or chives. Cover and let stand for several hours to blend flavors. Makes about 1 quart, or enough for 150 slices of bread.

Chilled crab salad nests in lettuce cups atop buttered bread rounds for Crab Salad Sandwiches.

Chicken Salad Sandwich

Here's another perky salad-topped sandwich.

2 quarts chopped cooked chicken or turkey
1 cup finely chopped celery
1 cup chopped cashews, pecans, or water
    chestnuts
1 cup mayonnaise
2 teaspoons seasoned salt
½ teaspoon curry or dill weed
2 tablespoons lemon juice
⅓ cup finely chopped radishes or green onion
1 jar or can (4 oz.) pimiento, cut in strips
50 sandwich bread slices
About ¾ cup soft butter
100 tiny lettuce cups or spears (butter lettuce
    or romaine)

Combine the chicken with celery, nuts, mayonnaise, seasoned salt, curry or dill, lemon juice, radishes or green onions, and half the pimiento (save rest for garnish). Chill until ready to serve. Cut each bread slice into 2 rounds or squares; spread each with butter. Top with tiny lettuce cup, romaine spear, or shredded lettuce. Spoon in a mound of the salad. Garnish each with small piece of pimiento. Makes 100.

Frosted Pimiento Cheese Rolls

These finger sandwiches are made from single slices of bread, spread and then rolled.

½ cup instant minced onion
1 cup water
1 cup soft butter or margarine
1 cup mayonnaise
4 quarts shredded American cheese
    (about 4 lbs.)
1 cup chopped pimiento (about 2 cans or jars,
    4 oz. each)
1½ cups finely chopped watercress or parsley
100 to 120 sandwich bread slices, crusts trimmed

Stir the onion into water, let stand for 5 minutes. Beat together the butter, mayonnaise, and cheese. Mix in the onion, pimiento, and watercress or parsley. Spread one side of each bread slice with cheese mixture until you have used about ⅔ of total amount. Roll each like a jelly roll. Place close together on baking sheets. Spread tops with remaining cheese mixture. Just before serving set into a moderately hot oven (350° to 375°) until rolls are deep golden brown, 10 to 12 minutes. Makes 100 to 120.

Pimiento Cheese Rolls are frosted with additional cheese mixture before they are toasted in oven.

Beef and Olive Sandwiches

Chipped beef, olives, and minced onion are the tasty flavorings in this filling.

2 tablespoons instant minced onion
⅓ cup dry sherry or chicken broth
1 quart (about 10 oz.) chipped beef
5 packages (8 oz. each) cream cheese
1 cup mayonnaise
1½ cups chopped stuffed green olives or ripe
    olives
60 slices thinly sliced sandwich bread

Stir onion into sherry; let stand for 5 minutes. Chop beef into small pieces. Soften cream cheese; blend in mayonnaise until smooth. Stir in the onion mixture, chipped beef, and olives. Spread on 30 slices of the bread; top with the remaining 30 slices of bread. Cut each large sandwich into thirds or quarters. Makes 90 to 120.

Seafood-Cucumber Filling

This filling is equally good in tiny tea sandwiches or in hearty full-sized sandwiches.

1 cup crab meat or chopped, cooked shrimp
⅓ cup grated or chopped peeled cucumber
2 teaspoons chopped green onion
1 to 2 teaspoons lemon juice
¼ teaspoon salt
⅛ teaspoon dried dill weed
4 tablespoons mayonnaise or sour cream

Combine crab, cucumber (press moisture out between paper towels or folds of a clean cloth), onion, lemon juice, salt, dill weed, and mayonnaise. Chill thoroughly. Makes about 1¼ cups.

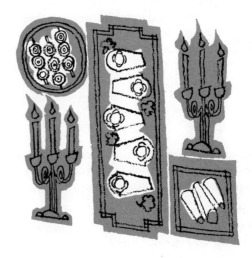

Guests serve themselves at sandwich buffet. After first course of small smørrebrød with hot soup, follow with main dish choice, then with dessert smørrebrød.

A SANDWICH BUFFET

The open sandwiches described here comprise a make-ahead guest meal you can serve on your patio. The idea came from Denmark, where the art of arranging delectable food combinations on thin slices of buttered bread originated. This menu combines three typical kinds of open sandwiches into a three-course party meal that includes first course, main course, and dessert. *Smørrebrød* is the Danish word for these creations. Each sandwich should be approached as a work of art in form and color as well as in flavor.

You can make the sandwiches up to three hours before serving them; arrange on trays, cover carefully with clear plastic wrap, and keep in refrigerator.

Before guests arrive, arrange a buffet table with soup cups or mugs and two sets of sandwich plates (one for the first course, one for the main course).

Also set individual places at small tables with knives, forks, napkins, and coffee cups. At serving time, bring the first course and main dish smørrebrød to the buffet table with hot soup; your guests serve themselves to these two courses. Later replace sandwich plates with small dessert plates, and pass dessert smørrebrød selection with hot coffee.

First Course

Make the soup ahead and reheat just before serving. Allow two or three smørrebrød for each guest; offer a variety of two or three kinds.

Dilled Green Pea Soup: Combine in a pan 2 packages (10 oz. each) frozen peas, 2 cans (14½ oz. each) chicken broth, ¼ teaspoon each salt and dried dill weed. Cook until tender, about 10 minutes. Whirl in a blender until smooth or press through a strainer. Reheat, stirring. Serve hot. Makes 6 servings.

Salmon with Cucumber: Arrange thin slices of cucumber on small round slices of buttered rye bread. Top each with thinly sliced smoked salmon (about 4 oz. for 6 smørrebrød) which you have rolled into a cylinder shape. Spoon whipped cream (for 6, beat 3 oz. package with 2 tablespoons milk) into open end of roll. Tuck in a few blades of chives.

Egg Salad on Tomato Slice: Arrange butter lettuce leaves on small round slices of buttered rye bread. Top each with a thin tomato slice and a spoonful of curried egg salad (for 6 sandwiches, mix 2 hard-cooked eggs, diced, ¼ cup diced celery, 4 teaspoons mayonnaise, ¼ teaspoon dry mustard, and salt and pepper to taste). Garnish with parsley sprigs.

Anchovy and Onion: Cut thin slices of firm white bread into 3-inch squares, removing crusts. Top each with a mound of sliced green onions with tops, 2 drained flat anchovy fillets, crossed, and a small spoonful of sieved, hard-cooked egg yolk.

Danish open-face sandwiches are knife-and-fork foods; set places for your guests at small tables.

rolled (about 10 oz. ham for 6 sandwiches). Top with a well-drained spiced peach half. Add a sprig of watercress just before serving.

Main Course Smørrebrød

Plan on about two sandwiches per guest. If you wish to simplify the menu, offer only two choices, or even just one kind.

Turkey Breast with Red Cabbage: Butter thin slices of firm white bread. Top each with overlapping thin slices of turkey breast meat (about ½ pound for 6). At one corner arrange a small cup of butter lettuce; fill with well-drained canned red cabbage, and top with sour cream and a piece of spiced watermelon rind.

Roast Beef with Horseradish Cream: Arrange butter lettuce leaves over buttered slices of rye bread. On each drape a large thin slice of rare roast beef (about 10 oz. for 6 sandwiches). Top with a tiny cup of butter lettuce filled with horseradish sour cream (for 6 smørrebrød, fold 1 teaspoon prepared horseradish into 6 tablespoons sour cream), and a few onion rings which have been deep-fried until golden and crisp.

Ham and Cheese with Spiced Peach: Butter thin slices of rye bread. At one end of each, arrange a leaf of butter lettuce topped with a few overlapping thin slices of Danish Tybo cheese or other mild natural slicing cheese (about 3 oz. for 6 sandwiches). At the other end arrange 2 thin slices of boiled ham,

Dessert Smørrebrød

Plan on two of these for each of your guests. Offer two or three kinds.

Blue Cheese with Cherries: Butter 3-inch squares of thin-sliced rye bread (crusts removed). Top each with overlapping thin slices of blue cheese (about 2 oz. for 6 smørrebrød) and a small spoonful of cherry preserves.

Cream Cheese with Apricots: Generously spread round butter puff wafers with softened cream cheese (two 3 oz. packages for 6). Top each with a fresh apricot half, a walnut half, and a small spoonful of red currant jelly.

Tybo Cheese with Marmalade: Butter crisp rectangular butter tea biscuits. Top with 2 thin slices Danish Tybo cheese or other mild natural slicing cheese (about 2 oz. for 6), a spoonful of orange marmalade, and a washed lemon blossom.

Cucumber Dill Sandwiches

These have the garden-fresh aroma of cucumber and dill.

Spread small rectangles of thinly sliced coarse-textured pumpernickel bread with soft butter. Cover with thinly overlapping unpeeled slices of cucumber (cut slices in half if cucumber is large). Sprinkle lightly with salt and dill weed.

Eight ways you can cut regular-sized double sandwiches to make three or four small finger sandwiches from each. Vary cutting to give assorted shapes.

Bacon-Watercress Sandwiches

You can make these a day in advance if you keep them tightly wrapped in clear plastic wrap or a damp cloth enclosed with foil.

4 large packages (8 oz. each) cream cheese or
    pimiento cream cheese
⅔ cup cream
2 tablespoons vinegar or lemon juice
1 teaspoon salt
1 pint chopped watercress
30 slices (about 1½ pounds) bacon, cooked
    crisp and crumbled
60 slices thinly sliced sandwich bread

Soften cream cheese. Beat in cream until mixture is smooth. Add vinegar or lemon juice, salt, watercress, and crumbled bacon. Mix well. Spread on 30 of the bread slices and top with remaining 30 bread slices. Cut some of the sandwiches into thirds and some into quarters, trimming crusts. Makes 90 to 120.

Gingered Fruit Sandwiches

Ginger, dates, and pecans flavor the cream cheese filling for these party sandwiches.

3 large packages (8 oz. each) cream cheese
½ cup cream or mayonnaise
3 tablespoons lemon juice
1 teaspoon seasoned salt
¼ cup finely chopped candied or preserved
    ginger
1 to 1½ cups finely chopped dates
½ cup finely chopped pecans or walnuts
60 slices thinly sliced sandwich bread

Soften cream cheese. Beat in cream, lemon juice, and seasoned salt. Add ginger, dates, and pecans or walnuts; mix well. Spread on 30 of the bread slices and top with the other 30 slices. Cut sandwiches into thirds or quarters. Makes 90 to 120.

Grilled Sandwich Miniatures

Here's an idea you can vary, using any piquantly flavored meat or fish sandwich filling in place of the liver sausage. You can make the sandwiches ahead, wrap, and refrigerate them, but spread outsides with butter and cut them into bite-sized sandwiches just before you grill them.

½ pound liver-flavored sausage (about 1 cup)
½ cup chili sauce
2 tablespoons chopped dill pickle
16 to 20 slices white bread
Soft butter or margarine

Combine sausage, chili sauce, and chopped pickle; mix well. Spread filling on half the bread slices; top with remaining bread slices. Trim crusts, keeping the sandwiches as square as possible. Spread soft butter or margarine on both top and bottom of sandwiches. Using a sharp knife, cut each large sandwich first into 4 triangles, then cut each again to make 8 small triangles. Use a wide pancake turner to lift each cut sandwich onto your preheated sandwich grill; close grill and cook until bread is toasted golden brown. Use turner again to lift sandwiches to a warm serving plate. Makes about 6 dozen miniature sandwiches.

Shrimp and Asparagus Sandwiches

Cut thin slices of firm white bread into 2 by 4-inch rectangles, removing crusts. Spread with butter, top each with a lengthwise row of small cooked shrimp, a spear of cooked and chilled asparagus cut to fit bread, and a piping of curry-seasoned mayonnaise pressed from a force bag.

Grilled Sandwich Miniatures: Sandwiches are pre-cut into bite-sized pieces before they are grilled.

Nasturtium Sandwiches

The nippy flavor of nasturtium is apparent in these very attractive tea sandwiches.

Spread small squares of thinly sliced coarse-textured pumpernickel or firm-textured rye bread with soft butter. Top each with a small washed and drained nasturtium leaf, stem removed, or washed and well drained nasturtium blossom. (You can mince the stems and blend with the butter as a spread for these sandwiches.)

INDEX

Photographers: Glenn M. Christiansen, pages 7, 9, 28, 37, 47, 54, 59, 74, 76, 81, 92, 93; Darrow M. Watt, pages 4, 11, 12, 13, 14, 16, 19, 24, 29, 30, 33, 34, 35, 38, 41, 43, 44, 53, 60, 62, 65, 66, 67, 69, 70, 72, 73, 75, 79, 83, 86, 88, 90, 91, 94, 95. **Illustrated by** Emery K. Mitchell.

Cover photograph: Papaya with prosciutto ham, salmon-cream cheese rolls (page 28), deviled eggs with almonds (page 28), cheese-stuffed celery, cherry tomatoes with smoked oysters (page 28). Photograph by Darrow M. Watt.